Dibyendu Choudhury

The Dark Web
A Web of Deceit

A Guide for Net Safety

Dibyendu Choudhury

Dedication

To my mother, who taught me to love reading and writing, to my family, who always encouraged me to pursue my dreams, and to all those who fell prey to deception, fraud, and harassment on the dark web, who motivated me to write this book and raise awareness about this hidden and dangerous world.

Foreword

The dark web can be a concern for everyone, including our loved ones. It's important to be aware that it can attract cybercriminals who may pose a threat to innocent individuals, like your caring old parents.

This book offers a fascinating look into the world of fraudsters and criminals, shedding light on how they exploit unsuspecting individuals. It tells the story of how my dear mother, unfortunately, fell for a tricky phone call from her bank during her retirement years, leading to the heartbreaking loss of her hard-earned money. This experience can be quite scary, and it's a reminder for the many people who encounter similar situations on a daily basis.

The dark web's anonymity can unfortunately attract some crafty individuals who engage in illegal activities such as drugs and weapons. This poses an ongoing danger to innocent people. These sneaky criminals like to use fake identities, which can make it tough for law enforcement to catch them. In addition, the dark web unfortunately allows hackers to sell personal information, which can greatly compromise the security and privacy of individuals. Therefore, it's really important for everyone to stay alert and learn about online scams and frauds in order to protect themselves from becoming victims of these sneaky tricks.

I don't want to freak you out with fear, just wanted to let you know that cybercrime is definitely something we should all be aware of. It's a growing threat that unfortunately affects millions of people worldwide on a daily basis. Stay safe out there! Hey there! I came across a report by Norton LifeLock that shared some interesting information. It turns out that in 2020, around 330 million people from 10 different countries, unfortunately, fell victim to cybercrime. Could you imagine it? In addition, they collectively lost more than $1 trillion. Clearly, this is a problem that we should all be aware of. Cybercriminals, unfortunately, target individuals of all ages, backgrounds, and geographic locations. Cybercriminals unfortunately target people from all walks of life, regardless of age, background, or location. However, they tend to focus on those who may be more vulnerable, such as seniors, children, and individuals with lower incomes. For instance, there was a situation where some cybercriminals pretended to be tech support representatives and targeted elderly individuals. They would give the victims a call and kindly persuade them that their computers might have viruses, encouraging them to grant remote access to their devices. Once given access, the criminals might install malware and take sensitive information, such as bank account details, which could lead to substantial financial losses for the victims. This example demonstrates how cybercriminals exploit vulnerable populations and employ psychological techniques to deceive and defraud individuals.

Just a friendly reminder to stay safe online. It's always a good idea to be cautious and avoid accepting friend requests or clicking on links from people or sources you don't know. Take care! Please remember to never share personal or financial information with anyone online. Please remember to avoid sending or receiving any explicit images or videos with anyone online. Make sure to always let your parents or guardians know before meeting someone in person. It's important to keep them in the loop for your safety.

Maintaining respect when posting or sharing anything on the internet is absolutely essential. Take a moment to consider whether you'd be comfortable with others seeing what you're about to share. Failure to do so could lead to serious consequences. Remember to always be mindful of what you say or do online, just as you would in real life. Please remember to avoid engaging in cyberbullying or sexting. Please remember to respect others' boundaries and avoid pressuring them into doing anything they're not comfortable with online.

Let's be smart! Make sure to use security software and privacy settings on your devices and online platforms to keep yourself safe! Remember to use strong passwords and make sure to change them regularly! It's always a good idea to use a VPN when you're connecting to public Wi-Fi networks. Stay safe and protect your online privacy! Remember to regularly back up your data!

If you come across any dubious activities or occurrences, it is crucial to promptly notify the appropriate authorities or organizations. Should you fall victim to cybercrime or abuse, it is recommended to seek assistance from reliable sources without hesitation. By following these helpful tips, younger people can greatly reduce their chances of falling victim to cybercrime and abuse. This way, they can fully enjoy the wonderful benefits of the internet while keeping their security and well-being intact. Young people can gain a better understanding of how to navigate the online world safely by being proactive and seeking guidance from trusted individuals.

Just wanted to remind you that reporting any suspicious activities or incidents is super important. Not only does it help keep you safe, but it also plays a big role in creating a safer online environment for everyone. So don't hesitate to report anything fishy you come across! By following these steps, young people can safely enjoy all the amazing opportunities the internet has to offer while keeping themselves protected from any potential risks.

This information should give you a comprehensive understanding of the challenges and opportunities that the Internet presents to young individuals. Should you require any assistance with content creation or writing, feel free to ask others whom you feel comfortable discussing.

Additionally, it's really important for parents, guardians, and educators to actively participate in educating young individuals about internet safety. By helping them understand the possible risks and showing them how to safely navigate the online world, we can empower them to make wise choices and keep themselves safe. We have the power to create a secure and welcoming online space that enables young people to thrive in the digital era. As responsible adults, parents can confidently set up parental controls on their children's devices and monitor their online behaviour to ensure they are not exposed to any unsuitable content or individuals. Furthermore, educators can confidently incorporate internet safety lessons into their curriculum to promote safe online behaviour. Let's work together to ensure the safety and well-being of our youth in the digital world. By teaching students about privacy settings, online etiquette, and the significance of verifying information before sharing it, they can help create a safer online environment. By getting involved in their online education, adults can really make a difference in helping young individuals develop critical thinking skills and feel confident about using the internet in a safe and responsible way. For instance, a teacher can help students by showing them how to analyze and evaluate online sources in a friendly way. They can teach them how to fact-check news articles or spot biases in social media posts to determine their credibility. In addition, educators have the opportunity to create simulations of real-life situations where students can practice making informed decisions. For instance, they can learn how to identify and avoid fraudulent emails and comprehend the risks associated with sharing personal information on social platforms.

Happy Surfing and stay safe.

Dr. Dibyendu Choudhury,

Date: 6th Aug 2023

Disclaimer

This book is intended to provide general information and guidance. It is not a substitute for professional advice or services. The author and the publisher do not guarantee the accuracy, completeness, or suitability of the information and opinions expressed in this book for any specific purpose or situation. The reader is advised to consult with a qualified professional before taking any action based on the contents of this book.

The author and the publisher are not responsible for any errors or omissions in this book or for any consequences arising from the use of this book. The author and the publisher do not endorse or recommend any products, services, websites, or organizations mentioned in this book. The views and opinions expressed in this book are solely those of the author and do not necessarily reflect those of the publisher or any other person or entity.

The author and the publisher have taken all reasonable care to ensure that the information and opinions in this book are current and accurate as of the date of publication. However, Internet Security and threats are ever-changing and evolving. Therefore, the reader is advised to verify the latest developments and updates before relying on any information or opinion in this book.

Table of Contents

INTRODUCTION

Introduction

The Hidden Layers of Deception

In the vast and enigmatic realm of the Dark Web, a labyrinthine network of deceit and malevolence awaits those who dare to explore its depths. This subchapter, aptly titled "The Hidden Layers of Deception," sheds light on the clandestine mechanisms that fuel the dark underbelly of the internet. As adults seeking knowledge and understanding, it is crucial to grasp the intricate web of deceit that permeates this murky domain.

A Web of Deceit

The Dark Web thrives on deception, fuelled by individuals and organized groups who are experts in manipulation. This subchapter explores the complex world of cybercrime, online schemes, and the strategies employed by these malicious actors. From phishing scams to identity theft, the reader will gain an understanding of the ingenious techniques used to exploit unwary victims. Understanding these deceptive strategies is the first step in avoiding falling victim to their pitfalls.

Cybersecurity and Online Scams

In an era in which technology has become an integral part of our lives, it is impossible to overstate the need for comprehensive cybersecurity measures. This subchapter examines the evolving landscape of cybersecurity, shedding light on the constant battle against hackers and cybercriminals. It explores the strategies employed by both individuals and organizations to safeguard their digital assets, providing readers with valuable knowledge to protect themselves from online scams and breaches.

Psychological Manipulation and Mind Control

The Dark Web is not only a breeding ground for cybercrime but also an unsettling arena for psychological manipulation and mind control. This subchapter delves into the sinister methods employed by malevolent entities to influence and control unsuspecting individuals. From online cults to psychological warfare techniques, readers will gain an understanding of the psychological vulnerabilities that can be exploited and how to defend against them.

Espionage and Intelligence Agencies

The hidden layers of deception extend beyond cybercrime and psychological manipulation; they reach deep into the realm of espionage and intelligence agencies. This subchapter uncovers the covert operations conducted by these shadowy organizations, exploring the intricate world of spies, moles, and double agents. Readers will gain a glimpse into the tactics employed by intelligence agencies and the lengths to which they go to protect national security.

As adults with a thirst for knowledge, it is crucial to recognize the hidden layers of deception that lurk within the Dark Web. By understanding the web of deceit, cybersecurity threats, psychological manipulation, and espionage tactics, readers can navigate this treacherous landscape with caution and protect themselves from the lurking dangers. By shedding light on these hidden layers, "The Dark Web: A Web of Deceit" aims to empower and educate its audience, equipping them with the knowledge needed to navigate the treacherous digital landscape.

ACE WEB
ryone
EVERYDAY
EVERYDAY
P WEB
SEMI BADI
ADVANCED
WEB
dden & inaccessible
dard browsers and
THREAT AC
NATION STA
BAD GUYS
INTRODUCTION TO
DARK WEB
Chapter-1

Chapter1: Introduction to the Dark Web

The Dark Web: A Web of Deceit

Enter the obscure world of the Dark Web, where secrecy is the standard, and illegal activities run rampant. This domain is a hub for deception, cybercrime, espionage, and manipulation, and we will explore its enigmatic realm.

The Dark Web is an encrypted network that exists within the deep recesses of the internet. Unlike the surface web, which is accessible to everyone through search engines, the Dark Web requires special software, such as Tor, to access its hidden sites. It is a parallel universe, a digital underworld where anonymity is the norm and identities are concealed behind layers of encryption.

There is a prevalence of cybersecurity threats and online scams within the Dark Web. This subchapter will explore the sophisticated techniques employed by cybercriminals to exploit unsuspecting victims. From phishing scams and ransomware attacks to identity theft and credit card fraud, the Dark Web is a breeding ground for malicious activities. Understanding the tactics employed by hackers and scammers is crucial to protecting oneself in an increasingly interconnected world.

But the Dark Web is not just about financial crimes; it is also a hub for psychological manipulation and mind control. This subchapter will shed light on the techniques used by manipulators to exploit vulnerable individuals. The internet's shadowy corners are rich with opportunities for psychological manipulation, ranging from social engineering and gaslighting to cult recruitment and brainwashing.

Intelligence agencies and espionage also have a presence in the Dark Web. Our focus will be on how these agencies monitor and infiltrate these covert networks. From state-sponsored cyber espionage to the recruitment of hackers for covert operations, the Dark Web has become a battleground for nations and intelligence agencies seeking to gain the upper hand in the world of digital warfare.

In this book, we will navigate the treacherous waters of the Dark Web, unveiling its secrets and exposing the web of deceit that lures unsuspecting individuals into its clutches. By understanding the inner workings of this hidden realm, readers will be better equipped to protect themselves from online threats, recognize psychological manipulation, and gain insights into the world of espionage and cyber warfare.

Join us as we navigate the treacherous waters of the internet, where truth is scarce and deception is constantly lurking. Get ready to delve into the enigmatic depths of the Dark Web, which is akin to an iceberg with only 33% explored and exploited while the other 67% remains uncharted. The individuals who operate in this realm are like pirates on the high seas, engaging in deceptive practices that will make you question everything you thought you knew about the internet and people's ability to manipulate it.

Origins and Development of the Dark Web

In the vast expanse of the internet lies a hidden realm, a subterranean underworld known as the Dark Web. This subchapter delves into the origins and development of this mysterious corner of the digital universe, exploring its emergence as well as its evolution into the complex network of deceit it is today.

The Dark Web, as we know it, can be traced back to the early 2000s. It was a time when the internet was gaining popularity, and cybercriminals sought new avenues to carry out their illicit activities away from prying eyes. The Dark Web's encryption tools and decentralized infrastructure provide anonymity, making it a haven for cybercrime to proliferate.

As the Dark Web began to take shape, it quickly became a hotbed for illegal activities, ranging from drug trafficking and weapon sales to hacking forums and identity theft. The emergence of Bitcoin, a decentralized digital currency, further facilitated transactions within this shadowy realm, making it easier for criminals to carry out their nefarious deeds without leaving a trace.

However, the Dark Web's development was not solely fuelled by criminal activities. Whistleblowers and activists also found solace in this hidden enclave, using it as a platform to expose corruption and challenge oppressive regimes. Individuals seeking to exchange information and ideas without any monitoring or censorship have found refuge in the Dark Web.

The Dark Web's expansion presented significant challenges to security agencies and intelligence organizations. The potential of this hidden realm was soon realized by espionage and intelligence agencies, who began utilizing it as a covert platform for their operations and intelligence gathering. The veil of anonymity provided by the Dark Web allowed agents to infiltrate criminal networks and collect critical intelligence without detection. However, the development of the Dark Web also led to new forms of psychological manipulation and mind control. Online scams and schemes thrived within this hidden world, preying on unsuspecting individuals and exploiting their vulnerabilities. Techniques of psychological manipulation like social engineering and phishing became more prevalent, luring victims into revealing personal information or falling for financial scams.

Today, the Dark Web is a multifaceted entity that continues to evolve. It serves as a hub for cybercriminals, intelligence agencies, activists, and individuals seeking refuge from the prying eyes of surveillance. Understanding the origins and development of the Dark Web is crucial for anyone interested in cybersecurity, online scams, psychological manipulation, or espionage.

In the following chapters, we will explore the various facets of this hidden realm, uncovering the web of deceit that underlies its existence. Brace yourself for a journey into the darkest corners of the internet, where anonymity reigns and deception thrive.

Understanding the anonymity behind it

In the vast landscape of the internet, there exists a hidden realm known as the Dark Web. It is a web of deceit, thriving on the anonymity it offers to its users. In this subchapter, we delve deep into the underbelly of the Dark Web to understand the intricate web of anonymity that shrouds it.

The Dark Web, unlike the surface web we are accustomed to, is not indexed by search engines and requires specific software to access. This veil of secrecy allows users to browse and engage in activities without revealing their true identities. It is a haven for cybercriminals, hackers, and those seeking to exploit others.

The Dark Web is infested with cybersecurity threats and online scams. Unscrupulous individuals take advantage of its anonymity to perpetrate illegal activities such as peddling pilfered personal information and carrying out illicit transactions. This cloak of anonymity shields them from law enforcement agencies and emboldens their criminal operations to flourish.

Despite the fact that criminals are not the only ones who reap the benefits of the anonymity provided by the Dark Web, intelligence agencies and espionage operatives also exploit this obscure realm to gather information, conduct covert operations, and monitor potential threats. The Dark Web becomes a breeding ground for espionage and counterintelligence, as agents manipulate the anonymity to their advantage.

The anonymous nature of the Dark Web closely associates it with psychological manipulation and mind control. With the ability to create multiple personas, individuals can easily deceive others and manipulate them for personal gain. The Dark Web becomes a psychological playground where unsuspecting individuals fall victim to these manipulative tactics.

Understanding the anonymity behind the Dark Web is crucial for anyone concerned about their online safety and security. It is crucial to have robust cybersecurity measures, maintain constant vigilance against online scams, and safeguard one's personal information. Furthermore, this book exposes the covert actions undertaken by intelligence agencies in utilizing the Dark Web to gather vital intelligence.

In conclusion, the anonymity behind the Dark Web is a double-edged sword. While it provides a haven for cybercriminals and facilitates espionage activities, it also serves as a reminder of the importance of vigilance and cybersecurity. To avoid falling prey to the enticing but deceptive aspects of the Dark Web, it's important to have a thorough understanding of the anonymity it offers and navigate the digital world with heightened awareness.

The Underbelly of Cybersecurity

The internet is a vast realm where anonymity rules and there is a dangerous underbelly that only a few are brave enough to explore. This subchapter of "The Dark Web: A Web of Deceit" delves deep into the sinister world of cybercrime, shedding light on the hidden dangers that lurk behind the veil of cybersecurity.

Cybersecurity, a term that invokes a sense of safety and protection, is not without its flaws. This subchapter explores how even the most sophisticated security measures can be breached by cunning individuals and organized criminal networks. Cybercriminals have become experts in exploiting vulnerabilities in digital security, ranging from infiltrating government databases to stealing private information from unsuspecting individuals.

In the realm of cyberspace, online scams are a grave menace. Their forms vary, ranging from false investment schemes that pledge unrealistic returns to phishing attacks that seek to thieve personal and financial data. These scams particularly target the susceptible and oblivious individuals. Additionally, we meticulously investigate the techniques employed by online scammers and expose the psychological manipulation and mind control tactics they utilize to dupe their prey. As regular individuals, we may not possess the knowledge or resources necessary to prevent an incident. Only after it occurs can we conduct a post-mortem analysis.

Espionage and intelligence agencies also find their place in this subchapter, as we explore how these shadowy organizations leverage the power of the internet to gather information, conduct covert operations, and manipulate geopolitical landscapes. From state-sponsored hacking to the nefarious activities of rogue intelligence agents, we uncover the dark side of cyber espionage and the potential threats it poses to national security.

As we explore the depths of cybersecurity, it is abundantly clear that the internet is no longer the safe haven it was once believed to be. The book thoroughly examines the vulnerabilities that exist within our digital infrastructure and underscores the urgent imperative for individuals, organizations, and governments to step up their cybersecurity measures.

This book "The Dark Web: A Web of Deceit" functions as a wake-up call for all adults who inhabit the digital world. It is a call to action, urging readers to educate themselves on the threats that lie beneath the surface and to take proactive measures to defend themselves from cyber threats. This subchapter endeavors to equip its audience with the knowledge, awareness, and tools necessary to navigate the treacherous waters of the internet safely by shedding light on the underbelly of cybersecurity.

Vulnerabilities exploited by cybercriminals.

The digital world is in a constant state of flux, and cybercriminals are experts at exploiting weaknesses to carry out their harmful deeds. These weaknesses, often overlooked or underestimated, are powerful tools for those who wish to create chaos, steal personal information, or harm individuals and organizations. In this section, we delve into the vulnerabilities that cybercriminals exploit, exposing the seedy underbelly of the internet.

A paramount danger exists due to the deficiency of knowledge and education amongst individuals. Countless online users fall prey to scams and phishing attacks due to their inability to recognize warning signs. Cybercriminals capitalize on this ignorance by exploiting psychological ploys to manipulate emotions and commandeer actions. By understanding the tactics employed by these criminals, individuals can arm themselves with the knowledge needed to recognize and avoid falling into their traps.

Another vulnerability lies within the realm of cybersecurity itself. Despite advancements in technology, hackers and cybercriminals constantly find new ways to breach security systems and gain unauthorized access to sensitive data. This vulnerability is particularly concerning for intelligence agencies and organizations dealing with classified information. Espionage and cyberattacks have become intertwined, with nation-states and criminal organizations using sophisticated techniques to infiltrate systems and steal valuable data. This subchapter explores the complex world of cyber-espionage and the devastating consequences it can have on national security.

In addition, cybercriminals have found a safe space for their unlawful actions with the emergence of the dark web. This hidden network of websites is not searchable via typical search engines and has become a hub for criminal activities such as drug and human trafficking, along with the sale of stolen data. This section aims to reveal the workings of the dark web and how it enables cybercriminals to carry out their actions with a sense of anonymity.

By uncovering and understanding these vulnerabilities, individuals, organizations, and intelligence agencies can better prepare themselves for the challenges posed by cybercriminals. Through education, cybersecurity measures, and increased awareness, we can create a safer digital environment and protect ourselves from falling victim to the web of deceit spun by cybercriminals.

The Tor Project, Inc. was established as a nonprofit organization in 2006, but the concept of "onion routing" was first initiated in the mid-1990s. Tor is the only browser that leads to this world, and its developers, researchers, and founders are a diverse group of individuals who share a common belief in the importance of private access to an uncensored internet.

During the 1990s, there was growing awareness of the internet's lack of security and its potential for tracking and surveillance. In 1995, David Goldschlag, Mike Reed, and Paul Syverson at the U.S. Naval Research Lab (NRL) pondered whether there was a way to create internet connections that could not be traced by network monitors. They developed the first onion routing research designs and prototypes to address this issue.

The goal of onion routing was to provide internet users with maximum privacy by routing traffic through multiple servers and encrypting it at each step. This remains a basic explanation of how Tor works today.

Types of online scams prevalent on the Dark Web

The Dark Web, with its hidden corners and encrypted communication channels, has become a breeding ground for various online scams. This subchapter will shed light on the most prevalent types of scams that thrive within its depths. From financial fraud to identity theft, cybercriminals employ sophisticated techniques to deceive unsuspecting individuals and organizations.

Phishing is a well-known type of online scam that operates on the Dark Web. This scam involves criminals impersonating credible entities to coax users into revealing sensitive information, such as their credit card details, usernames, or passwords. These scams often target individuals through emails, text messages, or even fake websites, exploiting their trust in well-known brands or institutions.

Another prevalent scam on the Dark Web is the sale of counterfeit goods. Cybercriminals take advantage of the anonymity provided by the Dark Web to set up online marketplaces where they sell counterfeit products, ranging from luxury items to pharmaceuticals. These scams not only defraud consumers but also harm legitimate businesses as they undermine their brand reputation and revenue.

Furthermore, the Dark Web is a hotbed for identity theft. Criminals exploit stolen personal information to commit various fraudulent activities, such as opening fraudulent bank accounts, applying for loans, or even committing financial crimes on behalf of unsuspecting victims. This type of scam can have devastating consequences for individuals, leading to financial ruin and damaged credit.

Psychological manipulation and mind control scams are also prevalent on the Dark Web. These scams target vulnerable individuals by exploiting their fears, desires, or insecurities. Scammers use psychological tactics to manipulate their victims into believing in false promises or engaging in harmful activities. These scams can have long-lasting effects on the mental well-being of the victims, leaving them traumatized and susceptible to further exploitation.

It is imperative to understand that the Dark Web serves as a platform for espionage and intelligence agencies to carry out their covert activities. State-sponsored hacking groups exploit the anonymity and encryption provided by the Dark Web to infiltrate systems, pilfer sensitive information, and conduct surveillance on targeted individuals or organizations. These activities pose a significant threat to national security, and their potential consequences can be far-reaching. It is crucial to remain vigilant and take proactive measures to prevent such malicious activity.

It is imperative that individuals and organizations remain vigilant on the constantly changing Dark Web. Awareness of the prevalent online scams is crucial in avoiding falling prey to cybercriminals. Familiarity with the tactics used by fraudulent schemers is the key to protecting oneself in this digital realm.

By raising awareness and implementing robust cybersecurity measures, we can collectively combat the web of deceit that exists within the dark underbelly of the internet.

The economics of cybercrime

The economics of cybercrime is a complex and ever-evolving topic that delves into the financial aspects of illicit activities conducted on the dark web. In this subchapter, we will explore the intricate web of deceit that fuels the world of cybercrime and shed light on the economic motivations behind these nefarious activities. Understanding the economics of cybercrime is crucial for adults who are interested in the dark web, cybersecurity, online scams, psychological manipulation, mind control, espionage, and intelligence agencies.

At its core, cybercrime is driven by profit. The dark web provides a platform for criminals to exploit the anonymity and untraceability it offers, allowing them to conduct illegal activities and monetize their endeavors. From hacking and identity theft to drug trafficking and counterfeit goods, cybercriminals have mastered the art of making money through illicit means.

There are different ways to study the economics of cybercrime. One approach is to analyze the costs and benefits for criminals, while another is to examine the impact on the global economy as a whole. Cybercriminals weigh the potential profits against the risks involved, including the chances of getting caught and the penalties they may face. The allure of financial gain often outweighs the potential repercussions, making cybercrime an attractive venture for many.

The dark web functions as a platform for cybercriminals to exchange and sell stolen data, hacking tools, and illegal merchandise. This underground economy operates through cryptocurrencies such as Bitcoin, which offer an extra level of secrecy. The use of digital currencies enables money laundering and allows cybercriminals to convert their unlawful profits into untraceable funds.

Furthermore, cybercrime has a significant impact on the global economy. The costs associated with cyberattacks, including financial losses, reputational damage, and increased cybersecurity measures, are staggering. Businesses and individuals alike bear the brunt of these economic consequences, as they invest in cybersecurity measures to protect themselves from the ever-increasing threat of cybercrime.

In order to effectively counteract the increasing danger of cybercrime, it is crucial for both individuals and organizations to comprehend the economic factors that drive it. By comprehending the motivations and financial incentives behind cybercriminal activities, we can develop robust cybersecurity strategies, raise awareness about online scams, and empower individuals to protect themselves from falling victim to psychological manipulation and mind control techniques employed by cybercriminals.

In addition, exploring the economics of cybercrime can provide insights into the world of espionage and intelligence agencies. The dark web serves as a breeding ground for state-sponsored hacking campaigns and cyber-espionage, where nations compete to gain a strategic advantage over their adversaries.

In conclusion, the economics of cybercrime is a fascinating and critical subject that intersects with various niches, including cybersecurity, online scams, psychological manipulation, mind control, espionage, and intelligence agencies. To create a safer online environment for individuals and organizations, it's important to delve into the economic incentives driving cybercriminal activities on the dark web. This understanding will help unravel the web of deceit and pave the way for effective countermeasures.

The Battle for Control

In the vast and treacherous realm of the dark web, where deceit and treachery thrive, a battle for control rages on. This subchapter delves into the intricate web of power struggles, espionage, psychological manipulation, and the relentless pursuit of dominance. Brace yourself, for this is a realm where cybersecurity is paramount, online scams lurk around every corner, and intelligence agencies operate in the shadows.

A Web of Deceit: The dark web is a breeding ground for deceit, a complex network of hidden websites and encrypted communication channels. It is a place where hackers, criminals, and shady individuals converge, all vying for control over their own illicit domains. Within this web of deception, a constant power struggle ensues as individuals and groups fight to establish supremacy over others. Deciphering the motives behind their actions can be a daunting task, but one thing is clear – control is the ultimate prize.

Cybersecurity and Online Scams: As unsuspecting users navigate the dark web, they become easy targets for cybercriminals and their elaborate scams. From phishing attacks to ransomware, these malicious actors exploit the vulnerabilities of individuals who may be unaware of the dangerous waters they tread. This battle for control extends beyond mere financial gain; it is a fight for dominance in the digital realm, where manipulation is the weapon of choice.

Psychological Manipulation and Mind Control: The dark web is not solely defined by its technological prowess; it is a realm where psychological manipulation thrives. Deep within its confines, individuals and organizations employ sophisticated tactics to control and influence others. This subversive manipulation often preys upon the vulnerabilities and fears of unsuspecting victims, leaving them trapped in a web of mind control. This chapter uncovers the chilling realities of psychological manipulation and its insidious impact on those who fall victim to its snares.

Espionage and Intelligence Agencies: The dark web serves as a haven for spies and intelligence agencies seeking to gather information and gain a strategic advantage. Within this shadowy realm, they engage in covert operations, infiltrating criminal networks and gathering sensitive data. This subchapter sheds light on the clandestine activities of these agencies, revealing the lengths they go to acquire control over the vast web of deceit.

In the battle for control, the dark web emerges as a battleground where cybersecurity, online scams, psychological manipulation, and espionage converge. This subchapter serves as a guide, shedding light on the multifaceted nature of this clandestine world. Brace yourself, for what lies ahead is a journey into the depths of deception and the struggle for supremacy.

Government efforts to combat cyber threats.

In an increasingly interconnected world, where cyber threats lurk around every corner, governments have taken significant steps to safeguard their nations from the perils of the digital realm. This subchapter delves into the government's tireless efforts to combat cyber threats and protect its citizens from the dark underbelly of the internet.

Governments across the globe have recognized the gravity of cyber threats and established robust cybersecurity frameworks to counteract them. These frameworks encompass a range of measures, including legislation, intelligence agencies, and international cooperation.

Legislation plays a pivotal role in empowering governments to combat cyber threats effectively. Laws have been enacted to criminalize cyber activities such as hacking, identity theft, and online scams. These legal frameworks act as deterrents, enabling law enforcement agencies to bring cybercriminals to justice swiftly.

Furthermore, governments have established specialized intelligence agencies to monitor and counter cyber threats. These agencies are equipped with cutting-edge technology and highly skilled personnel who gather intelligence on potential cyber threats and work tirelessly to neutralize them. By infiltrating hacker networks and identifying vulnerabilities, these agencies play a crucial role in safeguarding national security.

In the realm of international cooperation, governments have recognized the need to collaborate with one another to combat cyber threats. Cybersecurity agreements and information-sharing initiatives have been established to foster collaboration and ensure that collective efforts are made to address global cyber challenges. By sharing data on emerging threats and best practices, governments can enhance their cybersecurity capabilities and stay one step ahead of cybercriminals.

The fight against cyber threats extends beyond technical measures. Governments are also investing in public awareness campaigns to educate citizens about the risks associated with the online world. By promoting cybersecurity practices and highlighting the dangers of online scams and psychological manipulation, governments aim to empower individuals to protect themselves from cyber threats.

In conclusion, the government's efforts to combat cyber threats are multi-faceted and comprehensive. Through legislation, intelligence agencies, international cooperation, and public awareness campaigns, governments are working tirelessly to create a safe and secure online environment for their citizens. However, the battle against cyber threats is ever evolving, requiring constant adaptation and innovation to stay ahead of malicious actors. By staying vigilant and investing in robust cybersecurity measures, governments can continue to protect their citizens from the web of deceit that lies within the dark corners of the internet.

The role of international organizations in cybersecurity

The role of international organizations in cybersecurity is of utmost importance in today's interconnected world. As the internet becomes an integral part of our daily lives, the threat of cyberattacks and online scams looms large, prompting the need for a concerted global effort to combat these nefarious activities. This subchapter explores the role of international organizations in safeguarding our digital landscape and shedding light on the dark web's web of deceit.

International organizations such as Interpol, the United Nations, and the International Telecommunication Union (ITU) play a crucial role in addressing cybersecurity challenges. These organizations foster collaboration among nations, facilitating the sharing of information, best practices, and intelligence to tackle cyber threats effectively. Their efforts transcend national boundaries and underscore the importance of international cooperation in combating online scams and cyberattacks.

One of the key functions of these organizations is to establish international norms and guidelines for cybersecurity. They work towards creating a framework that promotes responsible behaviour in cyberspace, discourages cybercriminal activities, and ensures the protection of individuals and organizations from cyber threats. By setting standards and fostering dialogue, international organizations aim to create a safer digital environment for all.

Moreover, international organizations engage in capacity-building initiatives to strengthen the cybersecurity capabilities of nations. They provide technical assistance, training programs, and resources to help countries develop robust cybersecurity strategies, enhance their cyber defence mechanisms, and improve incident response capabilities. By empowering nations to protect their digital infrastructure, international organizations contribute to the collective global defence against cyber threats.

In addition to their role in cybersecurity, international organizations also delve into the realm of psychological manipulation and mind control. With the rise of social media platforms and the widespread dissemination of fake news, psychological manipulation has become a potent weapon in the hands of malicious actors. International organizations research and analyze these manipulative techniques, seeking to understand their impact on individuals and societies. By shedding light on these deceptive practices, they help individuals recognize and resist attempts to manipulate their thoughts and actions.

Furthermore, international organizations delve into the world of espionage and intelligence agencies. They monitor the activities of state-sponsored hacking groups and cyber mercenaries, exposing their tactics and strategies. By keeping a close eye on the activities of these actors, international organizations contribute to the global effort to counter cyber espionage, protect sensitive information, and safeguard national security.

In conclusion, the role of international organizations in cybersecurity is multifaceted. They work towards establishing international norms, fostering collaboration, and building capacity, all aimed at strengthening global cyber defences. Additionally, their efforts extend to understanding psychological manipulation and espionage, shedding light on these dark practices. As the digital landscape continues to evolve, the role of international organizations in cybersecurity remains crucial in safeguarding our online world and countering the ever-present web of deceit.

Ethical hacking and its impact on the Dark Web

In the murky depths of the internet lies a hidden realm known as the Dark Web—a breeding ground for criminal activities, illicit trades, and nefarious schemes. However, amidst the darkness, a glimmer of hope emerges in the form of ethical hacking, a practice that aims to combat the very same threats that plague this hidden underworld.

Ethical hacking, also known as white-hat hacking, is the authorized and legal process of penetrating computer systems and networks to identify vulnerabilities and patch them before malicious hackers exploit them. This subchapter explores how ethical hacking has made a significant impact on the Dark Web and its various niches, shedding light on its potential to combat cybercrime, protect individuals and organizations, and undermine the operations of criminal enterprises.

The Dark Web thrives on anonymity and secrecy, allowing criminals to engage in illicit activities without fear of detection. However, ethical hackers have managed to infiltrate this clandestine realm, collecting valuable intelligence and exposing hidden criminal networks. By harnessing their skills and knowledge, these ethical hackers have become a formidable force against cybercriminals, disrupting their operations, and dismantling their illicit marketplaces.

One of the key impacts of ethical hacking on the Dark Web is the exposure and takedown of online scams. These scams often prey on unsuspecting victims, luring them into financial traps or stealing their personal information. Ethical hackers, armed with their technical expertise, have identified and dismantled numerous scam operations, safeguarding innocent individuals from falling victim to these deceitful schemes.

Moreover, ethical hacking has played a crucial role in uncovering instances of psychological manipulation and mind control within the Dark Web. Criminal organizations exploit psychological vulnerabilities to manipulate individuals into performing illegal activities or divulging sensitive information. Ethical hackers have delved into the depths of these manipulative tactics, providing valuable insights into the psychological techniques employed by cybercriminals. This knowledge has enabled investigators to enhance their understanding of psychological manipulation, ultimately assisting in the development of strategies to counter such tactics.

Additionally, ethical hacking has unveiled the activities of espionage and intelligence agencies lurking within the Dark Web. State-sponsored cyber espionage poses a significant threat to national security, as intelligence agencies seek to gain access to classified information and disrupt rival nations. By infiltrating these covert operations, ethical hackers have not only exposed the activities of these agencies but have also helped governments bolster their cybersecurity defences, safeguarding valuable national assets.

In conclusion, ethical hacking has had a profound impact on the Dark Web, challenging the criminal underbelly that thrives within its depths. By leveraging their skills and knowledge, ethical hackers have disrupted cybercriminal operations, exposed online scams, unveiled psychological manipulation, and even undermined espionage activities. Their invaluable contributions have not only protected individuals and organizations but have also played a crucial role in the ongoing battle against cybercrime and deception in the digital age.

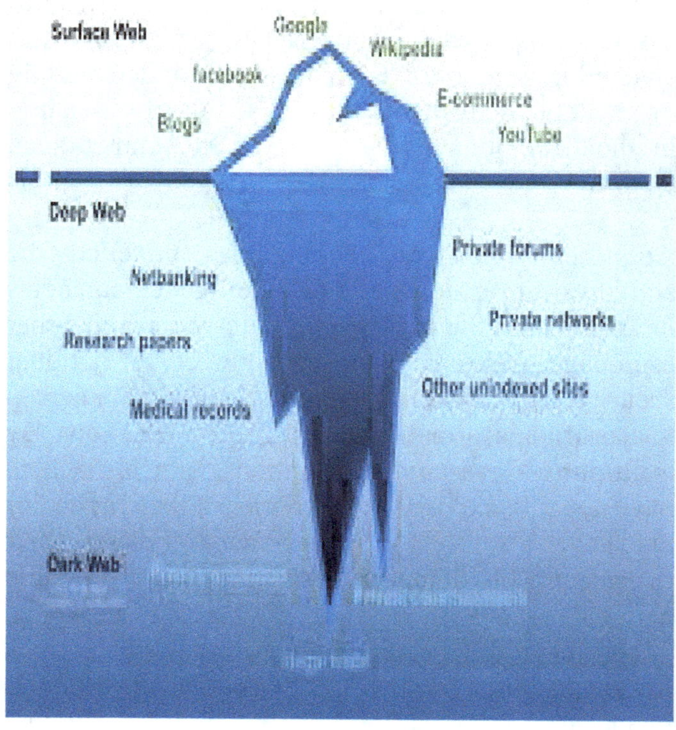

UNMASKING THE
WEB OF DECEIT
Chapter-2

Chapter 2: Unmasking the Web of Deceit

Psychological Manipulation: A Weapon of Choice

In the murky depths of the internet lies a sinister realm known as the Dark Web, where deception reigns supreme and unsuspecting victims fall prey to a web of deceit. This subchapter delves into the insidious world of psychological manipulation, a weapon of choice for those who thrive on exploiting the vulnerabilities of others.

In the realm of cybersecurity and online scams, psychological manipulation plays a pivotal role in ensnaring unsuspecting individuals. Cybercriminals employ a range of techniques, such as social engineering and mind control, to manipulate their victims into divulging sensitive information or carrying out malicious actions. By preying on human weaknesses, these manipulators can deceive even the most cautious and tech-savvy individuals.

Understanding the techniques used in psychological manipulation is crucial to safeguarding oneself against online threats. From the art of persuasion to the power of suggestion, manipulators exploit human psychology to gain control and advantage. By creating a false sense of trust or triggering emotional responses, they override rational thinking, leaving victims vulnerable to their devious schemes.

Espionage and intelligence agencies have long recognized the potency of psychological manipulation as a tool for gathering classified information and influencing political landscapes. From honey traps to brainwashing techniques, these clandestine operations employ psychological manipulation to infiltrate enemy lines, extract vital intelligence, and control the minds of their targets.

This subchapter also explores the ethical implications of psychological manipulation. While it can be employed for nefarious purposes, it is crucial to distinguish between its ethical and unethical applications. Understanding the boundaries of manipulation is essential to protect individuals from falling victim to its darker side and to promote responsible use within intelligence agencies and other domains.

By shedding light on the tactics and methodologies used by manipulators, this subchapter aims to empower readers to recognize and defend against psychological manipulation. Awareness is the first line of defence in the battle against online scams, deceit, and mind control. Only by understanding the depths to which manipulators will sink can we hope to navigate the treacherous waters of the Dark Web and emerge unscathed.

In conclusion, psychological manipulation is a formidable weapon in the arsenal of those who seek to exploit others. By studying its techniques and understanding its implications, we can arm ourselves against the dangers lurking in the shadows of the internet. Let us not be mere pawns in the game of deception, but rather informed individuals who stand strong against the web of deceit that threatens our cybersecurity, mental well-being, and the very fabric of our society.

Understanding the tactics employed by cybercriminals.

In the digital age, cybercriminals have become a formidable threat, lurking in the shadows of the internet, ready to exploit unsuspecting victims. In order to protect ourselves, it's crucial to have an understanding of the tactics utilized by individuals and organizations in the online world. This section will explore the dark side of the internet, shedding light on the methods used by cybercriminals to deceive, manipulate, and infiltrate our lives.

One of the most common techniques used by cybercriminals is phishing. This involves sending fraudulent emails or messages that appear to be from legitimate organizations, such as banks or government agencies. These crafty criminals aim to trick people into revealing sensitive information like passwords, credit card details, or social security numbers. By being aware of warning signs like suspicious URLs or bad grammar, internet users can avoid falling prey to their schemes.

Another tactic frequently used by cybercriminals is ransomware attacks. These involve encrypting a person's files and demanding payment in exchange for their release. This malicious software can gain access to computers through infected websites, email attachments, or even USB drives.

It is crucial to have robust antivirus software, regularly update systems, and avoid downloading files from unknown sources to protect against these attacks.

Cybercriminals rely heavily on psychological manipulation and mind control to extract personal information. They exploit our emotions and vulnerabilities, often by creating counterfeit social media profiles that appear trustworthy. Through seemingly innocent conversations, they extract sensitive information. It is crucial to recognize these manipulative techniques and protect ourselves from these cyber threats.

Intelligence agencies and espionage also utilize cybercrime tactics to gather sensitive information from individuals, companies, and even governments. These state-sponsored cyberattacks use sophisticated methods like spear phishing, where specific individuals are targeted with personalized messages to gain unauthorized access. To avoid becoming a victim, individuals must adopt strong passwords, two-factor authentication, and regularly monitor their online presence. Awareness of these techniques employed by intelligence agencies can help individuals take necessary precautions.

In conclusion, the tactics employed by cybercriminals are constantly evolving, making it crucial for individuals to stay informed and vigilant. By understanding techniques such as phishing, ransomware attacks, psychological manipulation, and the tactics utilized by espionage and intelligence agencies, we can fortify our defences and protect ourselves from falling into the web of deceit. With the right knowledge and proactive measures, we can navigate the online world with confidence, outsmarting cybercriminals at their own game.

Exploiting human vulnerabilities for malicious purposes

In the realm of cyberspace, where deceit and deception thrive, humans are often the weakest link. This subchapter aims to shed light on the dark underbelly of the internet, where malicious actors exploit human vulnerabilities for their nefarious purposes. Understanding these tactics is crucial for individuals interested in cybersecurity, online scams, psychological manipulation, mind control, espionage, and intelligence agencies.

The internet provides a fertile ground for cybercriminals to exploit human weaknesses. One such vulnerability is our innate trust in others. Cybercriminals capitalize on this by using social engineering techniques to manipulate individuals into revealing sensitive information, such as passwords or financial details. Through carefully crafted emails or phone calls, they deceive unsuspecting victims into believing they are interacting with a trusted entity, leading to devastating consequences.

Psychological manipulation is another potent weapon used by cybercriminals. By leveraging cognitive biases and emotional triggers, they manipulate individuals into making impulsive decisions that favour the attackers. Techniques like phishing, where fraudulent emails mimic legitimate organizations, exploit our fear of missing out or desire for instant gratification. These tactics are carefully designed to bypass our rational thinking and exploit our vulnerability to deception.

Espionage and intelligence agencies also employ human vulnerabilities to gather sensitive information. Covert agents exploit psychological weaknesses to recruit individuals with access to valuable intelligence. By preying on personal weaknesses, such as financial troubles or emotional distress, they manipulate targets into becoming assets for intelligence gathering, ultimately compromising national security.

It is crucial for people who want to safeguard themselves and their organizations from cyber threats to comprehend these tactics. By familiarizing oneself with the psychological methods employed by cyber criminals, individuals can improve their ability to be sceptical and think critically. Identifying the warning signs of phishing attempts, doubting the authenticity of requests for confidential information, and enforcing robust security protocols can greatly decrease the probability of experiencing cyber-attacks.

Moreover, intelligence agencies and security organizations must be well-versed in these techniques to protect national interests. By understanding the vulnerabilities that make individuals susceptible to manipulation, these agencies can enhance counterintelligence efforts, strengthen security protocols, and develop effective strategies to combat cyber threats.

To sum up, the dark web is a hazardous place where people's weaknesses are taken advantage of for harmful intentions. This section has examined the strategies used by cybercriminals, the manipulation tactics employed in online frauds, the significance of vulnerabilities in spying, and the crucial role of cybersecurity. By comprehending these ideas, individuals can better navigate the online world, being mindful and safeguarding themselves and their establishments from the hidden deceit that exists below the surface.

The psychology behind online scams

The psychology behind online scams is a captivating subject that sheds light on the dark underbelly of the internet. In this subchapter, we will explore the intricate web of deceit woven by cybercriminals, the psychological manipulation techniques they employ, and how intelligence agencies combat these threats.

Understanding the psychology behind online scams is crucial for individuals seeking to protect themselves in an increasingly interconnected world.

Cybersecurity is a pressing concern in today's digital age. The exponential growth of the internet has allowed scammers to exploit vulnerabilities, preying on unsuspecting victims. To truly comprehend the extent of this issue, it is essential to delve into the psychology of these criminals. They employ a range of tactics to manipulate their targets, exploiting basic human instincts such as trust, fear, and curiosity. By understanding how these psychological triggers are harnessed, individuals can better equip themselves against falling victim to online scams.

Online scams often involve psychological manipulation and mind control tactics to exploit cognitive biases and convince targets to give out sensitive information or make financial transactions. Scammers may use the authority bias or fear of missing out to persuade their victims. Recognizing and understanding these manipulation techniques can empower individuals to resist these tactics and protect themselves from scams.

When it comes to espionage and intelligence agencies, the psychology behind online scams becomes even more complex. State-sponsored hackers and cybercriminal organizations frequently use psychological tactics to infiltrate systems, gather intelligence, and disrupt adversaries. By researching the psychology behind online scams, intelligence agencies can effectively anticipate and counter these threats.

"The Dark Web: A Web of Deceit" this book offers a comprehensive exploration of the psychology behind online scams, providing insights into the motivations and techniques employed by cybercriminals. Drawing on real-life case studies and expert analysis, this subchapter delves deep into the minds of scammers, shedding light on their tactics and strategies.

Whether you are an individual seeking to protect yourself from online scams, a cybersecurity professional looking to enhance your knowledge, or an intelligence agency striving to stay ahead of the curve, understanding the psychology behind online scams is vital. By arming ourselves with knowledge, we can navigate the dark web with caution, preventing falling prey to the deception that lurks within its depths.

Mind Control: Unravelling the Techniques

In this subchapter, we delve into the chilling world of mind control, exposing the intricate techniques used to manipulate individuals and unravelling the sinister motives behind such tactics. From intelligence agencies seeking to gain an edge in espionage to cybercriminals aiming to exploit vulnerable individuals, the realm of mind control is a dark and treacherous one.

Understanding the psychological manipulation techniques employed by these malicious actors is essential for protecting oneself from their deceptive tactics. By illuminating these techniques, we hope to equip our readers with the knowledge required to identify and resist mind control attempts.

Gaslighting is one of the fundamental techniques used in mind control. This psychological manipulation entails subtly distorting a person's perception of reality in order to make them question their own sanity. To undermine a person's confidence in his or her own thoughts and emotions, perpetrators of gaslighting employ a variety of strategies, including denial, misdirection, and deliberate confusion.

Another method employed in mind control is the exploitation of cognitive biases. Our brains are wired to rely on mental shortcuts, or biases, to process information quickly. However, these biases can be exploited to manipulate our thoughts and actions. By understanding the various cognitive biases commonly exploited, such as confirmation bias and social proof, individuals can become more resistant to manipulation.

In this section, we will discuss the impact of technology on mind control. The growing reliance on digital platforms such as the internet and social media has made us vulnerable to cybercriminals who can manipulate our behaviour and exploit our weaknesses. To protect ourselves against these attempts at mind control, it is vital to understand how technology can be weaponized for targeted advertising and the spread of disinformation. Additionally, this section will examine intelligence agencies' use of mind control techniques for espionage purposes. By learning about these methods, we can gain insight into the shadowy world of espionage and the ethical implications of these actions, from the infamous MKUltra experiments to modern-day covert operations.

"Mind Control: Unravelling the Techniques" aims to equip our adult audience with the knowledge necessary to recognize and resist the insidious techniques used to manipulate and control. By shedding light on this dark web of deceit, we empower individuals to protect themselves and safeguard their mental autonomy in an increasingly interconnected world.

Social engineering and its impact on cybersecurity

Social engineering is a term used to describe a method of cyber-attack that relies on manipulating human psychology rather than exploiting technical vulnerabilities. It is a dangerous and increasingly prevalent tactic employed by cybercriminals and hackers to gain unauthorized access to sensitive information or deceive individuals into performing actions that may compromise their security.

In the realm of cybersecurity, social engineering presents a significant threat. It leverages psychological manipulation and mind control techniques to exploit human trust, curiosity, or fear. This subchapter explores the various techniques used in social engineering and its profound impact on cybersecurity.

One of the most prevalent ways cybercriminals deceive people is through phishing, where they send misleading emails or messages pretending to be a trusted source. These messages may include links or attachments that, when clicked, can result in downloading malware or sharing personal information. By impersonating a well-known organization, hackers exploit people's trust and create a sense of urgency to prompt immediate action.

Another type of social engineering is pretexting, where attackers create a false identity or scenario to trick victims into revealing sensitive information. This method takes advantage of human empathy and helpfulness, as the attacker could pretend to be a colleague, customer, or even a law enforcement officer. By establishing trust and credibility, the attacker can gain unauthorized access to secure systems or extract valuable data.

Social engineering is not only used for individual targets, but also by espionage and intelligence agencies on a larger scale. State-sponsored actors use these techniques to infiltrate organizations, governments, or institutions for the purpose of espionage or sabotage. By manipulating individuals within the target organization, attackers can gain access to classified information or compromise critical systems.

It is important to have an understanding of the psychology involved in social engineering in order to protect oneself from such attacks. People should be cautious when dealing with unsolicited requests or sharing personal information and should be aware of common tactics used in social engineering. Organizations must take measures to protect themselves, such as employee training, strict access controls, and multi-factor authentication. These steps help to reduce the risks associated with social engineering attacks.

In conclusion, social engineering poses a significant threat to cybersecurity. Its manipulation of human psychology and exploitation of trust make it a highly effective tool for cybercriminals, spies, and hackers. By staying informed and implementing robust security measures, individuals and organizations can better protect themselves against these deceptive tactics and safeguard their sensitive information.

Manipulative techniques used by cybercriminals.

Subchapter: Manipulative Techniques Used by Cybercriminals

Introduction:

In the vast and treacherous realm of the dark web, cybercriminals employ a wide array of manipulative techniques to deceive and exploit unsuspecting victims. This subchapter delves into the dark tactics employed by these malevolent individuals, shedding light on their methods of psychological manipulation, espionage, and mind control. By understanding these techniques, adult readers can arm themselves with knowledge to protect against online scams and cyber threats.

1. The Art of Social Engineering:

Cybercriminals have mastered the art of social engineering, exploiting the human tendency to trust and be helpful. They employ persuasive tactics such as phishing emails, impersonation, and fake websites to trick users into revealing sensitive information like passwords, credit card details, or personal identification numbers (PINs). By understanding these manipulative techniques, readers can become more vigilant and cautious when encountering suspicious online interactions.

2. Psychological Manipulation:

It is essential to comprehend the psychology behind cybercrime in order to combat online frauds. Cybercriminals manipulate their victims by exploiting cognitive biases such as fear, urgency, and authority. They create a sense of urgency by claiming immediate action is necessary to avoid repercussions or by impersonating authorities such as government agencies and financial institutions.

By investigating these manipulative techniques, readers can cultivate a critical mindset and become more resistant to psychological manipulation.

3. Espionage and Intelligence Agencies: The dark web serves as a hub for espionage and cyberattacks orchestrated by intelligence agencies worldwide. This subsection illuminates the techniques utilized by these agencies, such as hacking, espionage, and data intrusions. Understanding the methods employed in cyber espionage enables readers to comprehend the gravity of the threat and the significance of implementing robust cybersecurity measures.

As technology advances, cybercriminals develop increasingly sophisticated methods for exploiting victims who are unaware of their vulnerability. By examining the manipulative techniques employed by these individuals, the reader gains valuable insight into the web of deceit on the dark web. Armed with this knowledge, they will be able to improve their cybersecurity practices, identify online scams, and defend themselves from psychological manipulation. This subchapter is an indispensable resource for anyone interested in cybersecurity, online frauds, psychological manipulation, the world of espionage, and intelligence agencies. Maintain awareness and vigilance and navigate the digital world with care.

Protecting oneself from psychological manipulation

In the digital age, where anonymity prevails supreme, psychological manipulation poses a significant threat. The Dark Web, a breeding ground for deceit and cybercrime, has become a playground for manipulators and dictators. This subsection attempts to equip adults with the knowledge and tools necessary to avoid falling victim to such tactics.

Understanding the tactics employed by manipulators is crucial. They exploit vulnerability, playing on emotions and insecurities to gain control. By understanding their methods, you can better protect yourself. Recognize the signs of gaslighting, where manipulators distort your perception of reality, making you doubt yourself. Be aware of charm and flattery, as manipulators often use these tactics to win your trust and blind you to their ulterior motives.

In the realms of cybersecurity and online schemes, psychological manipulation occurs frequently. Social engineering techniques are employed by malicious actors to deceive individuals into divulging sensitive information or falling for fraudulent schemes. Be sceptical of unsolicited emails or communications requesting personal information in order to protect yourself. Check the legitimacy of websites and avoid suspicious links. You can reduce your risk of becoming a victim of cybercrime by exercising caution and vigilance.

To shield yourself from psychological manipulation, it is essential to cultivate a strong sense of self-awareness. Be in tune with your emotions and thoughts. Manipulators prey on those who are unsure of themselves or lack self-confidence. By developing a healthy sense of self-esteem and trust in your instincts, you become less susceptible to their tactics.

The intelligence and espionage communities are also well-versed in the arts of psychological manipulation and mental control. It is essential to be aware of potential hazards in our interconnected world. Protect your personal information by using robust passwords and updating them frequently. Encrypt your data and use two-factor authentication whenever possible to prevent data breaches.

In conclusion, in today's digital landscape, psychological manipulation protection is essential. You can fortify yourself against potential hazards by understanding the strategies employed by manipulators, being cautious in online interactions, and cultivating self-awareness. Knowledge is the key to maintaining your autonomy and safety in the fight against deception.

The Dark Side of Technology

In today's digital age, technology has become an integral part of our lives. From smartphones to social media platforms, we rely on these innovations for communication, entertainment, and even personal safety. However, beneath the surface of this seemingly bright and convenient world lies a sinister underbelly - the dark side of technology.

"The Dark Web: A Web of Deceit" explores the hidden dangers lurking within the vast realm of the internet, shedding light on the grim consequences of our increasing dependence on technology. This subchapter, "The Dark Side of Technology", delves into the darker aspects that have emerged due to the rapid advancement of digital tools and connectivity.

One prominent issue addressed within this subchapter is cybersecurity and online scams. As our lives become increasingly entwined with the digital realm, cybercriminals take advantage of the vulnerabilities that come with it. From phishing scams to identity theft, these online criminals exploit unsuspecting victims, causing financial ruin and emotional distress. This section offers valuable insights into how to safeguard personal information and navigate the treacherous waters of the internet.

Furthermore, the subchapter explores the psychological manipulation and mind control tactics employed by tech giants and social media platforms. Through the collection and analysis of personal data, these entities have the power to influence our thoughts, behaviours, and even political beliefs. By examining real-life case studies and expert analysis, readers gain a deeper understanding of the extent to which our minds are being manipulated and the potential ramifications for society as a whole.

Espionage and intelligence agencies also play a significant role in the dark side of technology. The subchapter provides an in-depth examination of how these entities leverage technology to spy on individuals, governments, and corporations. From state-sponsored cyberattacks to surveillance programs, the dark side of technology reveals a world where privacy is scarce, and every digital interaction is potentially monitored.

"The Dark Side of Technology" offers a sobering look into the hidden dangers that accompany our reliance on digital tools. It serves as a wake-up call to adult readers, particularly those interested in cybersecurity, online scams, psychological manipulation, and espionage. By understanding the risks posed by the dark side of technology, readers can better protect themselves and their loved ones in an increasingly interconnected world.

The use of artificial intelligence in cybercrime

The use of artificial intelligence in cybercrime is a chilling reality that poses a significant threat to our digital security. As technology continues to advance at an unprecedented pace, criminals are finding new and sophisticated ways to exploit it for their nefarious activities. In this subchapter, we will explore the dark underbelly of the internet and delve into how artificial intelligence is being harnessed by cybercriminals.

Artificial intelligence, with its ability to learn, adapt, and make decisions, has become an invaluable tool for cybercriminals. It enables them to automate their attacks, making them faster, more efficient, and harder to detect. With AI, hackers can develop intelligent malware that can bypass traditional security measures, exploit vulnerabilities, and infiltrate even the most secure networks.

One of the most concerning applications of AI in cybercrime is in phishing attacks. AI-powered phishing emails can mimic the writing style and tone of trusted individuals or organizations, making them virtually indistinguishable from genuine communications. This level of sophistication greatly increases the success rate of phishing attempts, as unsuspecting victims are more likely to fall prey to these convincing scams.

Moreover, AI is being utilized in the creation of deepfake videos and images, a technique that combines AI algorithms with facial mapping to manipulate visual content. This has alarming implications for psychological manipulation and mind control, as cybercriminals can use deepfakes to spread disinformation, blackmail individuals, or even impersonate high-profile figures for political or financial gain.

Espionage and intelligence agencies are not immune to the influence of AI in cybercrime either. State-sponsored hackers can leverage AI to conduct large-scale surveillance operations, gathering vast amounts of data on individuals or organizations. This information can then be used to target victims with highly personalized attacks, exploiting their vulnerabilities and compromising sensitive information.

To combat the rising threat of AI-powered cybercrime, it is vital for individuals and organizations to stay informed and proactive. Investing in robust cybersecurity measures, such as advanced threat detection systems and user awareness training, is crucial in safeguarding against these evolving threats. Additionally, collaboration between governments, cybersecurity experts, and technology companies is essential to developing effective strategies to counter the dark forces that exploit AI for criminal purposes.

In conclusion, the use of artificial intelligence in cybercrime presents a grave danger to our digital world. As technology continues to evolve, so too must our defenses against these ever-evolving threats. By understanding the capabilities and tactics of cybercriminals, we can equip ourselves with the knowledge and tools necessary to protect ourselves and mitigate the risks that AI poses in the realm of cybercrime.

The evolution of malware and its implications

In the ever-changing landscape of the digital world, the evolution of malware has become a pressing concern. From the early days of simple viruses to the sophisticated and destructive forms we see today, the implications of malware reach far beyond the realm of technology. As we delve into the dark underbelly of the web, it becomes apparent that our interconnectedness has given rise to a web of deceit with far-reaching consequences.

Cybersecurity and online scams have become a battleground between criminals and those striving to protect our digital lives. Malware has evolved from mere annoyances to powerful tools that can cripple entire systems, steal sensitive information, and hold individuals and organizations hostage. The implications of such attacks are vast, ranging from financial losses to the compromise of national security. As we navigate these treacherous waters, understanding the evolution of malware is crucial to fortifying our defenses.

However, the implications of malware extend far beyond technological concerns. Psychological manipulation and mind control have become alarming byproducts of this evolution. Malware has been weaponized not only to steal data but also to manipulate individuals on a psychological level. The ability to exploit vulnerabilities, prey on emotions, and control behaviour has given rise to a new type of warfare—one that takes place in the depths of the human mind. The implications of such manipulation are profound, as it undermines trust, distorts reality, and poses a threat to our very sense of self.

Espionage and intelligence agencies have also found themselves on the frontlines of this battle. The evolution of malware has enabled state-sponsored attacks designed to infiltrate foreign governments, gather classified information, and disrupt infrastructure. The implications of these cyber operations are far-reaching, with the potential to destabilize nations, sow discord, and compromise the integrity of democratic processes.

As we explore the dark web, it becomes clear that the evolution of malware has far-reaching implications that extend beyond the confines of technology. It is a web of deceit that affects us all, regardless of our awareness or involvement. Understanding the evolution of malware is crucial for individuals, organizations, and governments alike, as it is only through this understanding that we can hope to protect ourselves and navigate the treacherous waters of the digital world.

The future of cybersecurity against advanced threats

As we progress further into the digital age, the threat landscape is swiftly evolving, and so must our cybersecurity strategy. The rise of the dark web has spawned a new species of sophisticated threats that pose a substantial risk to individuals, organizations, and even nations. In this subsection, we will examine the future of cybersecurity and the means by which we can combat these sophisticated adversaries.

Utilizing cutting-edge technologies and techniques to exploit vulnerabilities, threats on the black web have become increasingly sophisticated. The motives behind these attacks can vary from state-sponsored cyber espionage to organized criminal networks, ranging from the theft of sensitive information to the disruption of critical infrastructure.

To effectively counter these threats, cybersecurity professionals must adopt a proactive and multi-layered defense strategy. Traditional security measures like firewalls and antivirus software are no longer sufficient. Artificial intelligence and machine learning algorithms are now being employed to detect and respond to threats in real-time, enhancing our ability to identify malicious activities and prevent data breaches.

However, the future of cybersecurity is not dependent solely on technological progress. Understanding the human element of these hazards is likewise essential. Psychological manipulation and mind control are essential weapons used by the dark web to exploit human vulnerabilities.

Educating individuals about the perils of online scams and raising awareness about the methods used by cybercriminals is crucial for bolstering our defenses.

Additionally, collaboration between intelligence agencies and cybersecurity professionals is essential. Espionage and intelligence agencies have unique insights into the motivations and capabilities of dark web-based threat actors. By exchanging intelligence and coordinating our efforts, we can remain one step ahead of our adversaries and thwart their operations.

The future of cybersecurity will be determined by both individuals and organizations. Implementing robust security protocols, updating software on a regular basis, and practicing good cyber hygiene are essential measures for defending against advanced threats. In addition, policymakers must give cybersecurity a high priority and allocate resources to support cybersecurity research and development.

The future of cybersecurity against advanced threats will necessitate a multifaceted approach as the dark web continues to evolve. The key to defending against the ever-increasing threats in the digital domain is a combination of technological advancements, a deeper understanding of human vulnerabilities, and increased collaboration. We can navigate the web of deceit and safeguard the digital future by remaining vigilant, informed, and proactive.

ESPIONAGE IN
THE DIGITAL AGE
http://
YOUR PASSWORD
Chapter-3

Chapter 3: Espionage in the Digital Age

Intelligence Agencies and the Dark Web

In the ever-changing internet landscape, the Dark Web remains a mystery enveloped in mystery and intrigue. It has become a breeding ground for cybercriminals, hackers, and unlawful activities. However, what many may not realize is that intelligence agencies from around the world have also set their sights on this shadowy aspect of the Internet.

Intelligence agencies, such as the CIA, MI6, and Mossad, have long recognized the Dark Web as a potentially valuable source of information. Its anonymity and untraceability make it a fertile ground for garnering intelligence on a wide range of illegal activities, such as terrorism, drug trafficking, and money laundering.

In order to infiltrate the Dark Web and gather intelligence, these agencies employ a variety of methods. They frequently create aliases and establish a presence on various forums and marketplaces in order to acquire the confidence of criminals and collect information. Through these covert operations, they are able to unearth useful information, disrupt criminal networks, and avert potential threats to national security.

However, the intelligence agencies' involvement in the Dark Web is not without controversy. Critics argue that their actions may infringe upon individual privacy and civil liberties. The very nature of the Dark Web, with its encrypted communications and hidden services, raises questions about the ethics and legality of intelligence agencies' activities.

Moreover, intelligence agencies' presence on the Dark Web has also led to concerns about the potential for abuse and manipulation. With their vast resources and capabilities, these agencies have the power to exploit vulnerabilities and engage in psychological manipulation and mind control. The Dark Web becomes a battleground for intelligence agencies seeking to gain an upper hand in the world of espionage.

The intersection of the Dark Web and intelligence agencies also highlights the constant cat-and-mouse game between cybercriminals and those tasked with protecting national security. As intelligence agencies develop new techniques to monitor and infiltrate the Dark Web, criminals adapt and evolve their methods to stay one step ahead.

In conclusion, the Dark Web has evolved into a battlefield where intelligence agencies from around the world compete in a high-stakes game of intelligence collection and disruption. While their presence on the Dark Web raises ethical and legal concerns, there is no denying their significance in combating cybercrime and preserving national security. The relationship between intelligence agencies and the Dark Web will unquestionably shape the future of espionage and cybersecurity as technology continues to advance.

The role of intelligence agencies in monitoring the Dark Web

The Dark Web has emerged as a breeding ground for illicit activities, including cybercrime, online frauds, and psychological manipulation, in the ever-changing landscape of the Internet. As society becomes more interconnected, effective monitoring and surveillance of this concealed realm have become of the utmost importance. This subsection examines the role of intelligence agencies in defending against the Dark Web's threats.

Intelligence agencies like the CIA, MI6, and NSA play a crucial role in monitoring the Dark Web and mitigating its potential hazards. These agencies are responsible for collecting and analyzing vast quantities of data using sophisticated technologies and techniques in order to identify and monitor criminal activity in this hidden portion of the internet.

National security protection is a primary objective of intelligence agencies, and the Dark Web poses a significant threat in this regard. The Dark Web provides a platform for cybercriminals to engage in activities such as drug trafficking, weapon sales, and money laundering, which can all be used to finance terrorist organizations or destabilize economies. By monitoring the Dark Web, intelligence agencies can collect useful information to disrupt criminal networks, dismantle illicit operations, and prevent potential attacks.

In the digital age, cybersecurity and online fraud are also significant concerns. The Dark Web is a marketplace for stolen information, hacking tools, and personal data. Intelligence agencies work relentlessly to identify and neutralize cybercriminals who exploit online vulnerabilities, protecting individuals and organizations from financial loss, identity theft, and reputational harm.

Intelligence agencies closely monitor another aspect of the Dark Web: psychological manipulation and mental control. On these covert platforms, malicious actors engage in activities such as propagandizing, recruiting for extremist ideologies, and psychological warfare. By monitoring these activities, intelligence agencies can gain insight into the tactics employed by these actors, allowing them to devise countermeasures and prevent manipulation.

Intelligence agencies have always been concerned with espionage, and the Dark Web has become a refuge for spies and informants. Intelligence agencies monitor the Dark Web in order to identify potential threats to national security, monitor the activities of foreign intelligence services, and safeguard classified information from falling into the wrong hands.

In conclusion, the crucial role of intelligence agencies in monitoring the Dark Web cannot be overstated. Their tireless efforts to gather intelligence, analyze data, and disrupt criminal activities are instrumental in safeguarding national security, countering cybercrime, protecting individuals and organizations, and preventing psychological manipulation and espionage. As the Dark Web continues to evolve, intelligence agencies must adapt their strategies and technologies to stay one step ahead of those who seek to exploit the hidden depths of the internet. Only through their vigilance can we hope to mitigate the risks and navigate the treacherous waters of the Dark Web.

Espionage techniques employed by government entities.

In the realms of intelligence and national security, governments have relied on a variety of espionage techniques for decades. These clandestine operations are an integral component of global national defense strategies. In this subsection, we will examine several government espionage techniques, casting light on the murky underbelly of international intelligence operations.

One of the most common techniques utilized by government intelligence agencies is human intelligence, or HUMINT. This involves the recruitment and deployment of human agents who infiltrate target organizations or countries, providing valuable information to their handlers. HUMINT agents may be diplomats, journalists, or even individuals with no official ties to the government. They employ various tactics, such as bribery, blackmail, or even seduction, to gain the trust of their targets and extract sensitive information. Honey trapping is one of the functions of them.

Another prevalent espionage technique is signals intelligence, or SIGINT. This involves intercepting and analyzing communication signals, such as radio transmissions, telephone calls, and internet data, to gather intelligence. Government entities employ sophisticated technologies and skilled analysts to monitor and decipher these signals. Through SIGINT, governments can uncover hidden agendas, track the movements of individuals or groups, and identify potential threats to national security.

In recent years, cyber espionage has emerged as a potent tool in the arsenal of government entities. Cybersecurity experts and intelligence agencies engage in hacking, data theft, and the manipulation of computer systems to gain unauthorized access to sensitive information. These operations, often carried out by highly skilled hackers backed by government resources, can have far-reaching implications, breaching the security of nations, corporations, and individuals alike.

Psychological manipulation and mind control techniques also play a significant role in the espionage tactics employed by government entities. By exploiting human vulnerabilities and cognitive biases, intelligence agencies can influence individuals or entire populations to act in ways that serve their interests. Techniques such as propaganda, disinformation campaigns, and covert psychological operations are used to shape public opinion, destabilize governments, or manipulate the outcomes of elections.

Espionage and intelligence agencies are a fascinating and unsettling aspect of our modern world. The techniques they employ are both sophisticated and ethically questionable, raising important questions about privacy, security, and the balance between national interests and individual rights. In the following chapters, we will delve deeper into the intricacies of these techniques, exploring real-world examples and the implications they have on our interconnected society.

The ethical debate surrounding surveillance.

The ethical debate surrounding surveillance is a topic of immense relevance in today's interconnected world. As technology advances and our lives become increasingly digitized, the line between privacy and security becomes blurred. In this subchapter, we will delve into the complex ethical considerations surrounding surveillance practices, shedding light on the implications they have on individuals, society, and democracy itself.

Surveillance, both online and offline, is often justified as a means to safeguard national security and prevent acts of terrorism or cybercrime. Intelligence agencies argue that monitoring communications and gathering data is crucial for identifying potential threats. However, this approach raises concerns about the extent to which our privacy is invaded. Is it acceptable for governments and corporations to have access to our personal information, browsing habits, and even our most intimate conversations?

Critics argue that widespread surveillance infringes upon our fundamental rights, such as freedom of speech and the right to privacy. They contend that such practices create a chilling effect on individuals, stifling dissent and discouraging free expression. Furthermore, the vast amount of data collected can be misused or fall into the wrong hands, leading to identity theft, blackmail, or even psychological manipulation.

Psychological manipulation and mind control are not new concepts, but the digital age has provided new tools for those seeking to exploit vulnerable individuals. The information gathered through surveillance can be used to manipulate public opinion, influence elections, or spread propaganda. In an era where misinformation spreads like wildfire, this raises significant ethical concerns.

Espionage and intelligence agencies also play a central role in the surveillance debate. While these agencies are tasked with protecting national security, the methods they employ often infringe upon the privacy of both individuals and foreign governments. The line between legitimate intelligence gathering and illegal spying becomes increasingly blurry, leaving citizens and foreign entities at the mercy of powerful surveillance apparatuses.

As we navigate the treacherous waters of the dark web, cybersecurity and online scams add another layer to the ethical debate. The very tools designed to ensure our protection can be exploited by hackers and criminals, compromising our personal and financial security. The question arises: Do the potential benefits of surveillance outweigh the risks it poses to our privacy and security?

In conclusion, the ethical debate surrounding surveillance is a multifaceted issue with profound implications for individuals, society, and democracy. Striking the balance between privacy and security is a delicate task that requires careful consideration and robust safeguards. As we explore the dark web and its web of deceit, it is crucial to critically examine the ethical implications of surveillance practices in the digital age.

Cyber Espionage: Nation-State Threats

In the ever-evolving landscape of the digital world, the threat of cyber espionage looms large, with nation-states engaging in covert online activities to gain strategic advantages and compromise the security of other nations. This subchapter aims to shed light on the dangerous realm of nation-state cyber threats, exposing the tactics employed by intelligence agencies and their impact on individuals and societies.

Within the dark corners of the internet, where anonymity reigns supreme, nation-states engage in a sophisticated game of cyber espionage. Governments employ highly skilled hackers to infiltrate foreign networks, steal sensitive information, and disrupt critical infrastructure. These activities are not only limited to stealing military secrets or government intelligence but also extend to economic and trade espionage, targeting industries and businesses to gain a competitive edge.

The consequences of nation-state cyber threats are far-reaching. Not only do they compromise national security, but they also pose a significant risk to individuals and organizations. Advanced persistent threats (APTs) are employed by state-sponsored hackers to gain unauthorized access to systems and maintain a long-term presence, making detection and mitigation incredibly challenging. This subchapter will explore some of the most notable cyber-attacks, such as Stuxnet and the alleged Russian interference in the 2016 US presidential election, highlighting the extent of damage that can be inflicted through these covert operations.

Additionally, the psychological manipulation and mind control techniques employed by intelligence agencies to deceive and manipulate individuals will be examined. From targeted disinformation campaigns to social engineering tactics, these covert operations aim to manipulate public opinion, sow discord, and destabilize governments. The impact of such manipulations on societies and the erosion of trust in institutions will be discussed.

Furthermore, this subchapter will delve into the role of cybersecurity in countering nation-state cyber threats. It will explore the measures individuals, businesses, and governments can take to protect themselves from these sophisticated attacks. From implementing robust security protocols to cultivating a cybersecurity-conscious culture, understanding the importance of proactive defense mechanisms is crucial in this digital age.

In conclusion, this subchapter sheds light on the vast and complex world of nation-state cyber threats. By understanding the tactics employed by intelligence agencies, the psychological manipulation techniques utilized, and the steps necessary to safeguard against these threats, individuals and societies can better navigate the dark web of cyber espionage.

State-sponsored cyber-attacks and their objectives

In this subchapter, we delve into the world of state-sponsored cyber-attacks and their sinister objectives. With the rise of the Dark Web and the increasing sophistication of cyber threats, it has become imperative to understand the motivations behind these state-sponsored attacks.

State-sponsored cyber-attacks refer to malicious activities orchestrated by governments or intelligence agencies to gain unauthorized access to computer systems, networks, and critical infrastructure. These attacks are often executed with the aim of achieving strategic, political, or economic advantages. Understanding their objectives can shed light on the potential consequences and implications for individuals, organizations, and even nations.

One of the primary objectives of state-sponsored cyber-attacks is espionage. Intelligence agencies employ cyber operations to gather sensitive information, such as classified government documents, military strategies, or trade secrets. By infiltrating foreign networks, these agencies can acquire valuable intelligence that can be used for political leverage, economic advantage, or military superiority. The anonymity and global reach of the internet make it an ideal platform for covert operations, allowing cyber spies to remain undetected and untraceable.

Another objective of state-sponsored cyber-attacks is psychological manipulation and mind control. By infiltrating social media platforms, spreading disinformation, or manipulating online narratives, governments can shape public opinion, incite social unrest, or even sway elections. The goal is to control the information flow and influence the thoughts and behaviour of targeted populations. In an era where online platforms have become the primary source of news and information, these cyber-attacks pose a significant threat to the integrity of democratic processes and the stability of societies.

Furthermore, state-sponsored cyber-attacks aim to undermine the cybersecurity of targeted nations and organizations. By exploiting vulnerabilities in computer systems and networks, governments can disrupt critical infrastructure, cause economic damage, or compromise national security. These attacks can range from ransomware attacks on hospitals and utilities to sophisticated hacking operations targeting defense contractors or financial institutions. The objective is to weaken the targeted entity and gain a strategic advantage in the event of a conflict or negotiation.

In conclusion, state-sponsored cyber-attacks pose a grave threat to individuals, organizations, and nations. Whether driven by espionage, psychological manipulation, or the desire to undermine cybersecurity, these attacks have far-reaching consequences. It is crucial for individuals and governments to remain vigilant, enhance cybersecurity measures, and collaborate internationally to combat this growing menace. By understanding the objectives behind state-sponsored cyber-attacks, we can better protect ourselves and our societies from the web of deceit that lurks in the shadows of the Dark Web.

Case studies of cyber espionage incidents

In this subchapter, we delve into the intriguing world of cyber espionage, exploring real-life case studies that shed light on the methods, motives, and consequences of these malicious activities. Cyber espionage refers to the covert gathering of sensitive information, often by state-sponsored or criminal organizations, through the use of advanced cyber techniques. The incidents we will examine are a testament to the growing threat posed by this dark realm of the internet and its impact on individuals, organizations, and even nations.

One notable case study is the Stuxnet worm, discovered in 2010. This highly sophisticated malware, allegedly developed by the United States and Israel, targeted Iran's nuclear facilities. Its primary goal was to sabotage the uranium enrichment process, causing significant setbacks to Iran's nuclear program. Stuxnet showcased the potential power of cyber espionage, highlighting how a carefully crafted digital weapon could disrupt physical infrastructure.

Another captivating incident is the attack on the Democratic National Committee (DNC) during the 2016 U.S. presidential election. This cyber intrusion, attributed to Russian hackers, resulted in the leakage of sensitive emails and confidential information. The subsequent media frenzy and the impact on the election highlighted the far-reaching consequences of cyber espionage in the realm of politics and national security.

Moving beyond nation-state attacks, we explore the case of the Carbanak gang, a cybercrime organization responsible for one of the largest bank heists in history. Through meticulously planned spear-phishing campaigns and malware deployment, they managed to infiltrate financial institutions worldwide, stealing hundreds of millions of dollars. This case demonstrates how cyber espionage techniques can be employed for financial gain, blurring the lines between traditional espionage and cybercrime.

Lastly, we examine the sophisticated cyber espionage campaign known as GhostNet, attributed to Chinese state-sponsored actors. GhostNet targeted government organizations, embassies, and NGOs, aiming to infiltrate their networks and gather sensitive information. This case study sheds light on the geopolitical dimensions of cyber espionage, highlighting the role of nation-states in these activities and the potential impact on international relations.

These case studies offer a glimpse into the complex world of cyber espionage, where intelligence agencies, criminal organizations, and state-sponsored actors operate in the shadows. By understanding the motives, techniques, and consequences of these incidents, individuals and organizations can better protect themselves from the ever-evolving threats of the digital age.

The impact of cyber warfare on international relations

The threat of cyber warfare looms large in today's interconnected world, where technology has become an integral part of our existence. As nations become more reliant on digital infrastructure, the potential for disruption and chaos resulting from cyberattacks has emerged as a significant concern in international relations. This subchapter will examine the far-reaching effects cyber warfare has on the international stage.

Cyberwarfare is a new battlefield where traditional norms of engagement are no longer applicable. Cyberattacks can be conducted remotely, surreptitiously, and with plausible denial, unlike conventional warfare. This makes it difficult to attribute attacks to a specific nation and blurs the distinction between state-sponsored and non-state-sponsored attacks. This ambiguity has significant effects on international relations, as it becomes increasingly difficult to hold nations accountable for their actions in the cyberspace.

The consequences of cyber warfare are far-reaching and extend beyond mere disruptions to digital infrastructure. They can have severe economic, political, and social implications. For instance, a well-coordinated cyber-attack on critical infrastructure, such as power grids or financial systems, could plunge a nation into chaos, leading to economic collapse and social unrest. Such attacks can also compromise national security by stealing sensitive information or disrupting military command and control systems.

Cyberwarfare has an impact on international relations that extends beyond imminent damage. It can erode trust and cooperation among nations, leading to heightened tensions and the possibility of escalation. Fear of retaliation or reprisal from cyberattacks can impede diplomatic efforts and exacerbate existing conflicts. In addition, the asymmetrical nature of cyber warfare enables weaker nations to level the playing field by targeting the vulnerabilities of stronger adversaries, resulting in power shifts and realignments within the international order. Furthermore, cyber warfare has given rise to a new breed of espionage and intelligence gathering. State-sponsored hacking groups can infiltrate foreign governments, steal classified information, and gain an upper hand in negotiations. This has led to a digital arms race, with nations investing heavily in offensive and defensive cyber capabilities to protect their interests.

Cyberwarfare has a profound and multifaceted influence on international relations. It challenges traditional notions of warfare, diminishes the distinction between state and non-state actors, and poses serious threats to national security and stability. As nations navigate this treacherous terrain, it is essential to bolster cybersecurity measures, cultivate international cooperation, and establish norms and rules governing cyber behaviour in order to mitigate the risks posed by this new front in the war on terror.

Battling in the Shadows: Countering Espionage

The art of gathering covert information, espionage, has been a part of human history for centuries. Cyber espionage has emerged as a new form of espionage in today's digital age, in which the Internet has become an integral part of our existence. As we navigate the web's shadowy nooks and crannies, we must be vigilant and conscious of the lurking dangers.

In "The Dark Web: A Web of Deceit," we delve into the intricacies of cyber espionage and examine countermeasures for this clandestine activity. This subchapter illuminates the ever-changing world of intelligence agencies, their tactics, and the protective measures we can take.

The first line of defense against espionage is cyber security. It includes a variety of measures, including robust passwords, encryption, firewalls, and antivirus software. As individuals living in the digital age, we must remain vigilant in protecting our personal and professional data. By employing best practices and keeping abreast of the most recent security threats, we can reduce the likelihood of cyber espionage.

However, espionage transcends technological limitations. It borders on psychological manipulation and mental control. Intelligence agencies utilize techniques such as social engineering and psychological profiling to exploit human vulnerabilities. Recognizing and countering their efforts requires a firm grasp of these strategies. By recognizing our own biases and remaining sceptical of suspicious interactions, we can avoid falling victim to psychological manipulation.

Furthermore, being knowledgeable about the world of espionage empowers us to identify signs of covert activities. From detecting surveillance devices to recognizing the telltale signs of a mole, we can enhance our ability to spot and report espionage activities. By doing so, we contribute to the collective effort of safeguarding our societies against threats that lurk in the shadows.

"The Dark Web: A Web of Deceit" aims to equip adults with the knowledge and tools necessary to navigate the treacherous landscape of espionage. By understanding the tactics employed by intelligence agencies and staying vigilant in our online interactions, we can protect ourselves and our communities from the web of deceit that surrounds us.

In conclusion, countering espionage requires a multi-faceted approach. From bolstering our cybersecurity defenses to being aware of psychological manipulation techniques, we can fortify ourselves against the threats posed by espionage. By embracing this knowledge, we become active participants in the battle against those who seek to exploit and deceive. Together, we can create a safer digital world.

Strategies for detecting and preventing cyber espionage.

In this subsection, we will examine the numerous strategies that individuals, organizations, and intelligence agencies can use to detect and prevent cyber espionage. As the dark web continues to evolve and cyber threats become more sophisticated, it is imperative that we remain one step ahead in order to safeguard our sensitive data.

Establishing strong cybersecurity measures is one of the most effective strategies. This includes consistently updating software, implementing two-factor authentication, and encrypting data. In addition, organizations should conduct vulnerability assessments and penetration testing on a regular basis to identify any potential system vulnerabilities.

Educating individuals on the methods employed by cybercriminals is an additional crucial strategy. By increasing awareness of common online frauds and phishing attempts, individuals will be better able to recognize and avoid falling victim to these schemes. Employees can be educated about the significance of cybersecurity and best practices for protecting sensitive data through programs and seminars.

Collaboration and the sharing of information are also essential in the struggle against cyber espionage. To remain ahead of evolving threats, intelligence agencies and organizations should establish strong relationships and share threat intelligence. By combining their resources and knowledge, they can identify and neutralize potential cyber threats.

Furthermore, investing in advanced technology, such as artificial intelligence and machine learning, can significantly enhance cybersecurity efforts. These technologies can help in detecting suspicious activities, identifying patterns, and quickly responding to potential cyber threats.

Psychological manipulation and mind control techniques are often used by cybercriminals to deceive individuals and gain unauthorized access to their information. Therefore, it is essential to educate individuals about these tactics and equip them with strategies to resist manipulation. This can include teaching critical thinking skills, promoting media literacy, and encouraging cautious online behaviour.

Lastly, espionage and intelligence agencies need to stay vigilant and adapt to the changing landscape of cyber threats. By constantly updating their techniques and tools, they can effectively counter cyber espionage attempts. Regular audits and monitoring of networks, as well as conducting comprehensive background checks on employees, can help identify potential insider threats.

Detecting and preventing cyber espionage requires a multifaceted approach that combines robust cybersecurity measures, education and awareness, collaboration, advanced technology, and vigilance. By implementing these strategies, individuals, organizations, and intelligence agencies can better protect themselves against the dark web's web of deceit.

Collaboration between intelligence agencies and private sector

Collaboration between intelligence agencies and the private sector is a crucial component in the fight against cyber threats and online scams. In the dark recesses of the web, where deceit reigns supreme, this collaboration becomes even more imperative. Addressing the adult audience fascinated by the intricate web of deceit, cybersecurity, online scams, psychological manipulation, and espionage, this subchapter of "The Dark Web: A Web of Deceit" sheds light on the symbiotic relationship between intelligence agencies and private entities.

In today's interconnected world, intelligence agencies are confronted with an ever-evolving landscape of cyber threats. The private sector, with its technological expertise and vast resources, becomes an indispensable ally in combating these challenges. By pooling their resources and sharing knowledge, intelligence agencies and private entities can effectively identify and neutralize cybercriminals, safeguarding individuals, businesses, and even nations.

Cybersecurity and online scams have become a pervasive menace, targeting unsuspecting individuals and exploiting their vulnerabilities. The collaboration between intelligence agencies and the private sector enables the development of robust defense mechanisms, ensuring the protection of sensitive data and thwarting the machinations of cybercriminals. This collaboration involves sharing threat intelligence, conducting joint investigations, and implementing proactive measures to stay one step ahead of the perpetrators.

Psychological manipulation and mind control techniques have found a new breeding ground in the dark corners of the web. By collaborating with the private sector, intelligence agencies can tap into the expertise of psychologists and behavioural scientists, unravelling the intricate ways in which individuals are influenced and manipulated. This knowledge is then used to develop countermeasures, empowering individuals to recognize and resist such manipulations, ultimately safeguarding their mental well-being.

Espionage and intelligence agencies have long been associated with cloak-and-dagger operations. However, in the digital age, the collaboration between intelligence agencies and the private sector takes on a new dimension. Private entities possess vast amounts of data and technological capabilities, which, when combined with the expertise of intelligence agencies, can uncover hidden patterns, identify potential threats, and safeguard national security.

Collaboration between intelligence agencies and the private sector is instrumental in navigating the treacherous landscape of the dark web. By harnessing their collective strengths, these entities can unveil the web of deceit, fortify cybersecurity defenses, combat online scams, unravel psychological manipulation, and safeguard national security. The symbiotic relationship between intelligence agencies and the private sector is an essential pillar in the fight against cyber threats and the preservation of truth and security in our interconnected world.

Balancing national security and individual privacy

In an era where our lives are increasingly intertwined with the digital realm, the delicate balance between national security and individual privacy has become a pressing concern. This subchapter aims to shed light on the complex issues surrounding this topic, exploring the intricate web of deception spun by the dark corners of the internet.

As we delve into the depths of the dark web, we find ourselves navigating a treacherous landscape, where malicious actors lurk in the shadows, preying on unsuspecting victims. The constant threat of cyber-attacks, online scams, and identity theft looms large, endangering not only individuals but also the very fabric of our society. However, as we strive to protect ourselves from these perils, the question arises – at what cost?

The tension between national security and individual privacy becomes particularly pronounced when we consider the methods employed by intelligence agencies. In the pursuit of safeguarding our nations from potential threats, these agencies often resort to surveillance tactics that encroach upon our personal lives. The line between protecting the greater good and violating our fundamental rights becomes blurred, leaving us to ponder the true extent of our freedom in the digital age.

Moreover, the dark web serves as a breeding ground for psychological manipulation and mind control. It is here that cybercriminals master the art of exploiting vulnerabilities and manipulating human behaviour for their nefarious purposes. The power to influence the masses through targeted propaganda and disinformation campaigns poses a significant threat to both individuals and the stability of nations. The ability to strike a balance between an open society and protection against such manipulation becomes paramount.

Educating individuals on the methods employed by cybercriminals is an additional crucial strategy. By increasing awareness of common online frauds and phishing attempts, individuals will be better able to recognize and avoid falling victim to these schemes. Employees can be educated about the significance of cybersecurity and best practices for protecting sensitive data through programs and seminars.

Collaboration and the sharing of information are also essential in the struggle against cyber espionage. To remain ahead of evolving threats, intelligence agencies and organizations should establish strong relationships and share threat intelligence. By combining their resources and knowledge, they can identify and neutralize potential cyber threats.

UNRAVELLING
THE WEB
Chapter-4

Chapter 4: Unravelling the Web

The Dark Web: A Double-Edged Sword

Beyond the surface of the Internet, the Dark Web is a realm shrouded in secrecy and mystique. It has captured the imaginations of many, serving as fertile ground for both criminal and clandestine operations. In this subchapter, we will examine the duality of the Dark Web and how it cuts through the social fabric like a double-edged weapon.

At first glimpse, the Dark Web appears to be a haven for cybercriminals and those seeking to exploit naive users. It is a breeding ground for online scams, with readily available stolen credit card information, hacking tools, and illicit drugs. It is extremely difficult for law enforcement agencies to track and apprehend these criminals due to the anonymity afforded by the Dark Web. As we delve deeper into the world of cybercrime, we find that online scams can have detrimental effects on both individuals and businesses.

However, the Dark Web is not exclusively a criminal domain. It is also utilized by intelligence agencies and espionage operations. Behind the encrypted barriers of the Dark Web, governments and intelligence agencies collect data, conduct surveillance, and engage in clandestine activities. In the world of espionage, the capacity to operate undetected gives these organizations an unprecedented advantage. We will investigate the intriguing world of intelligence gathering and its ethical ramifications.

Beyond the domains of cybersecurity and espionage, the Dark Web possesses an additional sinister capability: psychological manipulation and mind control. Extremist ideologies, sects, and radicalization thrive in such an environment. Individuals can be lured into these dangerous echo chambers, where their beliefs are reinforced and their actions are manipulated, due to the anonymity afforded by the Dark Web. We will examine the psychological techniques employed by these groups as well as their far-reaching effects on society.

In this subsection, we will expose the complex web of deceit that the Dark Web has woven. Cybercrime, espionage, psychological manipulation, and mind control will be traversed. It is a voyage that will illuminate the hidden dangers that lurk beneath the surface of the internet and force us to question our own vulnerability in this digital age. Join us in this enlightening exploration of the Dark Web, where truth and deception are intertwined.

The advantages and disadvantages of anonymous networks

Subchapter: The Advantages and Disadvantages of Anonymous Networks

In the depths of the internet lies a shadowy realm known as the Dark Web, where anonymity reigns supreme. This subchapter delves into the advantages and disadvantages of anonymous networks, shedding light on the implications they hold for individuals and society as a whole.

Advantages:

1. Privacy Protection: Individuals can use anonymous networks to browse the Internet without revealing their actual identities. This is especially advantageous for those living under oppressive regimes or for those who value their privacy.

2. Secure Communication: Anonymity enables encrypted and untraceable communication, making it harder for malicious actors to intercept sensitive information. This advantage proves invaluable for whistleblowers, journalists, and activists who need to exchange information discreetly.

3. Circumventing Censorship: Anonymous networks provide a means to bypass government censorship and access restricted content. This allows individuals to exercise their freedom of speech and obtain information that would otherwise be inaccessible.

4. Protection Against Online Scams: By hiding personal information, anonymous networks reduce the risk of falling victim to online scams and identity theft. This advantage is particularly relevant for those engaging in financial transactions and sharing sensitive data online.

Disadvantages:

1. Criminal Activities: The veil of anonymity offered by these networks attracts nefarious actors who engage in illegal activities such as drug trafficking, human trafficking, and cybercrime. This dark underbelly of the anonymous web poses a significant threat to society.

2. Psychological Manipulation: Anonymous networks can serve as breeding grounds for psychological manipulation and mind control. Individuals may fall prey to scams, misinformation, and extremist ideologies, leading to radicalization and harm to themselves or others.

3. Espionage and Intelligence Agencies: Anonymous networks provide a haven for spies and intelligence agencies to operate covertly, collecting sensitive information for nefarious purposes. This poses a significant challenge to national security and international relations.

4. Lack of Accountability: The absence of accountability within anonymous networks can lead to a culture of impunity, where individuals feel free to engage in illegal or harmful activities without fear of consequences. This undermines the principles of justice and social order.

In conclusion, while anonymous networks offer undeniable advantages such as privacy protection and secure communication, they also present significant disadvantages. The dark side of these networks, characterized by criminal activities, psychological manipulation, and espionage, cannot be overlooked. As society navigates the intricate web of deceit, finding a balance between privacy and security becomes paramount in order to mitigate the potential risks associated with anonymous networks.

The impact of the Dark Web on society

The impact of the Dark Web on society is a topic that has grown increasingly relevant in recent years. As technology continues to advance, so do the threats lurking in the shadows of the internet. In this subchapter, we will explore the various ways in which the Dark Web has affected our society and delve into the dark underbelly of this hidden realm.

One of the most pressing concerns surrounding the Dark Web is its role in facilitating cybercrime. Criminals exploit the anonymity provided by the Dark Web to engage in illegal activities such as drug trafficking, weapon sales, and identity theft. This poses a significant challenge for law enforcement agencies worldwide, as tracking down these criminals becomes increasingly difficult.

Moreover, the Dark Web has become a breeding ground for online scams. From fraudulent investment schemes to counterfeit products, the Dark Web offers a safe haven for scammers to operate with impunity. Innocent individuals fall victim to these scams, losing their hard-earned money and sometimes even their identities. The impact on the victims can be devastating, both financially and emotionally.

Psychological manipulation and mind control are also prevalent on the Dark Web. Manipulative tactics, such as social engineering, are employed to exploit individuals' vulnerabilities and coerce them into divulging sensitive information. This psychological warfare can have far-reaching consequences, as victims may find themselves trapped in a web of deceit, unable to escape the clutches of their manipulators.

Espionage and intelligence agencies also find the Dark Web to be a valuable tool for their clandestine activities. The anonymity it provides allows spies to communicate and exchange sensitive information without fear of detection. This poses a significant threat to national security, as it becomes increasingly challenging to monitor and prevent potential threats.

In conclusion, the Dark Web's impact on society cannot be underestimated. It has given rise to a web of deceit, where cybercrime, online scams, psychological manipulation, and espionage thrive. As we navigate the digital landscape, it is crucial that we remain vigilant and take precautions to protect ourselves and our society from the dangers that lurk in the shadows of the Dark Web.

Future challenges and potential solutions

As we delve deeper into the dark underbelly of the internet, it becomes crucial to address the future challenges that await us. The world of the dark web is constantly evolving, and with it come new threats and potential dangers. In this subchapter, we will explore some of these challenges and propose potential solutions to combat the web of deceit that engulfs us.

One of the most pressing challenges is the ever-increasing sophistication of cybercriminals and their ability to exploit vulnerabilities in our online security. As technology advances, so does the arsenal of tools at their disposal. We must remain vigilant and adopt robust cybersecurity measures to protect our personal information and financial assets. This includes using strong, unique passwords, regularly updating our software, and being cautious of suspicious emails or links.

Another challenge lies in the realm of psychological manipulation and mind control. The dark web serves as a breeding ground for individuals who excel in using psychological techniques to manipulate others. From social engineering to grooming vulnerable individuals, these tactics can lead to devastating consequences. Education and awareness are key here. By understanding these manipulation techniques, we can better protect ourselves and our loved ones from falling victim to such schemes.

Espionage and the activities of intelligence agencies are also a significant concern in the dark web landscape. State-sponsored hacking and cyber warfare have become increasingly prevalent, with governments around the world engaging in covert operations to gain an edge over their adversaries. To counter this, international cooperation and collaboration between intelligence agencies are essential. Sharing intelligence and working together to develop advanced defensive strategies will be crucial in mitigating the threats posed by these activities.

In terms of potential solutions, there is no one-size-fits-all approach. However, a multi-pronged strategy combining technological advancements, legislative reforms, and public awareness campaigns can go a long way in combating the web of deceit. Investing in cutting-edge cybersecurity tools and research, implementing stringent laws to prosecute cybercriminals, and educating the public about the risks involved are vital steps.

Ultimately, the future challenges presented by the dark web are complex and ever evolving. However, by remaining proactive, informed, and united, we can strive to create a safer online environment. It is only through constant adaptation and collaboration that we can hope to keep the web of deceit at bay and protect ourselves from the sinister forces that lurk in the shadows of the digital world.

Navigating the Shadows: Protecting Yourself

In this subchapter, we delve into the critical topic of safeguarding oneself while treading the treacherous terrain of the Dark Web. As we explore the depths of this clandestine realm, it becomes imperative to equip ourselves with the necessary knowledge and tools to protect against the various threats lurking in the shadows. Whether you are a curious explorer, a cybersecurity professional, or someone seeking insights into the world of psychological manipulation and espionage, this chapter is designed to arm you with crucial information to navigate the Dark Web safely.

Cybersecurity and online scams are omnipresent pitfalls in the digital landscape. The Dark Web, being a hotbed for illegal activities, poses even greater risks. We discuss the various scams and fraudulent schemes that plague this hidden realm, shedding light on the techniques employed by cybercriminals to deceive unsuspecting victims. By understanding these tactics, readers can better identify suspicious activities and protect themselves from falling prey to online scams.

The Dark Web is not only a breeding ground for cybercriminals but also a haven for psychological manipulation and mind control. We delve into the techniques employed by malicious actors to exploit vulnerabilities in human psychology, such as social engineering and manipulation tactics. By understanding these nefarious strategies, readers can fortify their psychological defenses and recognize attempts to manipulate their thoughts, emotions, and actions.

Espionage and intelligence agencies also play a significant role in the Dark Web ecosystem. We explore the intricate connections between the Dark Web and intelligence agencies, shedding light on the covert operations that take place in this shadowy realm. By understanding the modus operandi of these agencies, readers can better comprehend the implications and potential risks associated with engaging in certain activities within the Dark Web.

Furthermore, this subchapter also unveils essential tools and practices to ensure personal safety while exploring the Dark Web. We discuss the significance of using virtual private networks (VPNs), secure browsers, and encryption techniques to safeguard one's online identity and protect sensitive information. Additionally, we provide guidance on adopting effective habits to maintain anonymity and reduce the risk of exposure to cyber threats.

Navigating the Shadows: Protecting Yourself is an indispensable guide for anyone venturing into the Dark Web. By arming yourself with the knowledge and tools outlined in this subchapter, you can confidently explore this shadowy realm while safeguarding your personal and digital well-being. Stay informed, stay vigilant, and stay safe in the face of the Dark Web's web of deceit.

Tips and techniques for staying safe online.

In this digital age, where the internet has become an integral part of our lives, it is crucial to be aware of the potential dangers that lurk within the depths of the online world. The Dark Web, with its web of deceit, cybercrime, psychological manipulation, and espionage, poses significant threats that can compromise our security and privacy. However, armed with the right knowledge and techniques, we can navigate this treacherous landscape with caution and protect ourselves from falling victim to online scams, cyberattacks, and mind control. Here are some essential tips for staying safe online:

1. Update your software and devices regularly: Regularly updating your operating systems, antivirus software, and applications helps protect against known vulnerabilities and ensures that you have the latest security patches.

2. Use strong, unique passwords: Create complex passwords that include a combination of upper and lowercase letters, numbers, and symbols. Avoid using the same password across multiple platforms.

3. Enable two-factor authentication: Two-factor authentication adds an extra layer of security by requiring a second verification step, such as a unique code sent to your mobile device, in addition to your password.

4. Be cautious of phishing attempts: Watch out for suspicious emails, messages, or calls asking for personal information. Avoid clicking on links or downloading attachments from unknown sources.

5. Practice safe browsing habits: Avoid visiting suspicious websites or clicking on unfamiliar links. Be wary of pop-up ads, as they may contain malware or lead to malicious websites.

6. Be mindful of your social media presence: Adjust your privacy settings to limit the amount of personal information visible to the public. Be cautious about sharing sensitive information or accepting friend requests from unknown individuals.

7. Educate yourself about online scams: Stay informed about the latest online scams and tactics used by cybercriminals. Be sceptical of offers that seem too good to be true and avoid sharing personal or financial information with unknown parties.

8. Use secure Wi-Fi connections: Avoid using public Wi-Fi networks for sensitive activities, such as online banking or shopping. If necessary, use a virtual private network (VPN) to encrypt your data and protect your privacy.

9. Regularly back up your data: Create backups of your important files and documents to protect against data loss in case of a cyberattack or hardware failure.

10. Trust your instincts: If something feels off or suspicious, trust your gut instinct. If a website or an email seems untrustworthy, err on the side of caution and avoid engaging with it.

By following these tips and practicing good online hygiene, you can minimize the risk of falling prey to the dark underbelly of the internet. Remember, staying safe online requires constant vigilance and an understanding of the ever-evolving tactics employed by cybercriminals.

Recognizing and avoiding online scams

In the age of the internet, our lives have become increasingly intertwined with the digital world. From shopping to banking and socializing, we rely heavily on online platforms for various tasks. However, this growing reliance has also given rise to a darker side of the web - a breeding ground for scams and fraudulent activities. In this subchapter, we will explore the world of online scams, learn how to recognize them, and equip ourselves with the tools to avoid falling victim to these deceitful traps.

Online scams come in various forms, from phishing emails and fake websites to social media scams and online dating frauds. They often prey on our vulnerabilities, exploiting our trust, and manipulating our emotions. It is crucial to be aware of the red flags and warning signs that can help us identify these scams.

One common tactic scammers use is psychological manipulation. They exploit our fear, greed, or curiosity, enticing us to divulge personal information or make financial transactions. By understanding these manipulative techniques, we can better protect ourselves from falling into their traps. This subchapter will delve into the psychological aspects of scams, shedding light on how scammers use mind control techniques to influence their victims.

Furthermore, we will examine the role of espionage and intelligence agencies in combating online scams.

As technology advances, so do the techniques employed by scammers. Intelligence agencies play a vital role in tracking down and dismantling scam operations. By understanding their efforts, we gain insight into the bigger picture of online security and the global fight against cybercrime.

To avoid falling victim to online scams, we must adopt a proactive approach. This subchapter will provide practical tips and strategies to protect ourselves online. From creating strong passwords and enabling two-factor authentication to avoiding suspicious websites and emails, we will explore the best practices for safeguarding our personal and financial information.

By the end of this subchapter, readers will have a comprehensive understanding of online scams, the psychological tricks scammers use, and the steps they can take to protect themselves in the digital realm. Empowered with this knowledge, they can navigate the web of deceit with confidence, ensuring their online experiences are secure and scam-free.

Secure practices for protecting personal information.

In today's digital age, where personal information is constantly at risk of being compromised, it is crucial for adults to be well-informed about secure practices for protecting their personal information. This subchapter aims to guide readers through the intricacies of safeguarding their data in an increasingly deceptive online world.

The Dark Web: A Web of Deceit serves as a wake-up call, shedding light on the dangers lurking in the shadows of the internet. As cybercriminals continue to evolve their tactics, it is necessary for individuals to stay one step ahead. This subchapter will equip readers with essential knowledge and practical strategies to fortify their online security.

The first step in protecting personal information is to understand the common vulnerabilities that cybercriminals exploit. From phishing attacks to social engineering, this subchapter will delve into the methods employed by hackers to gain access to sensitive data. By understanding these tactics, readers will be better equipped to recognize and avoid falling victim to online scams.

Building on this foundation, the subchapter will then guide readers through a comprehensive set of secure practices. Topics such as password management, encryption, and two-factor authentication will be covered in detail. Additionally, the importance of keeping software and devices up to date to mitigate potential vulnerabilities will be emphasized.

Psychological manipulation and mind control are powerful tools that cybercriminals use to exploit human vulnerabilities. This subchapter will explore the psychological tactics employed by online scammers and offer guidance on how to recognize and resist these manipulations. By understanding the psychological aspect of cybercrime, readers can better protect themselves and their personal information.

Furthermore, as espionage and intelligence agencies increasingly employ sophisticated techniques to gather information, this subchapter will provide insights into the potential risks faced by individuals. It will offer practical advice on how to safeguard personal information from government surveillance and protect privacy rights.

"Secure Practices for Protecting Personal Information" is a subchapter that caters to the audience of "The Dark Web: A Web of Deceit" book, focusing on the niches of A Web of Deceit, Cybersecurity and Online Scams, Psychological Manipulation and Mind Control, and Espionage and Intelligence Agencies. By immersing readers in the world of online deception, this subchapter aims to empower them with the knowledge and tools necessary to protect their personal information in an ever-evolving digital landscape.

The Call for Awareness and Action

In the age of technological advancements, the dark web has emerged as a breeding ground for deceit and malevolence. It is a hidden realm where cybercriminals and malicious entities lurk, preying upon unsuspecting victims. This subchapter, titled "The Call for Awareness and Action," aims to shed light on the urgent need for vigilance and proactive measures in the face of this growing menace.

A Web of Deceit exposes the intricate network of cybercrime that operates within the dark web. It reveals the alarming extent to which individuals and organizations fall victim to online scams, identity theft, and financial fraud. This chapter serves as a wake-up call to adults, urging them to recognize the gravity of these threats and take immediate action to protect themselves and their loved ones.

One of the key aspects highlighted in this subchapter is the critical need for enhanced cybersecurity measures. With the ever-increasing sophistication of hackers and their ability to breach even the most secure systems, it is imperative for individuals and businesses alike to invest in robust cybersecurity protocols. From encrypting personal data to adopting multi-factor authentication, this chapter provides practical tips and guidelines to fortify one's online defenses.

Furthermore, The Dark Web: A Web of Deceit delves into the realm of psychological manipulation and mind control. It explores how cybercriminals exploit human vulnerabilities, using techniques such as social engineering and phishing to gain unauthorized access to sensitive information. By understanding the tactics employed by these malevolent actors, readers can equip themselves with the knowledge needed to detect and thwart such attempts.

Espionage and intelligence agencies also play a significant role in the dark web's web of deceit. This subchapter delves into the murky world of state-sponsored hacking and cyber warfare. It sheds light on the tactics employed by intelligence agencies to gather information, infiltrate systems, and manipulate public opinion. By understanding the motivations and methods of these agencies, readers gain a deeper appreciation for the complex landscape of cybersecurity and the importance of safeguarding national security interests.

In conclusion, "The Call for Awareness and Action" serves as a rallying cry to the adult audience. It emphasizes the need for heightened awareness, proactive steps, and collective action to combat the web of deceit that thrives within the dark web. By embracing cybersecurity measures, staying vigilant against online scams, understanding psychological manipulation, and recognizing the impact of espionage and intelligence agencies, individuals can reclaim their control in the digital realm and protect themselves from the pervasive threats that lurk in the shadows.

Advocacy for cybersecurity education and awareness

In an era where the internet has become an integral part of our lives, it is crucial to understand the importance of cybersecurity education and awareness. The digital world we live in is rife with dangers, ranging from cybercrime to psychological manipulation. This subchapter aims to shed light on the urgent need for advocacy in the realm of cybersecurity, targeting the adult audience interested in topics such as online scams, psychological manipulation, espionage, and intelligence agencies.

The Dark Web: A Web of Deceit explores the hidden underbelly of the internet, where criminals lurk and exploit unsuspecting victims. However, this subchapter delves deeper into the solution rather than dwelling solely on the problem. It advocates for cybersecurity education and awareness as the ultimate defense against the threats that plague the digital landscape.

Cybersecurity education empowers individuals with the knowledge and skills necessary to protect themselves online. By understanding the tactics employed by cybercriminals, individuals can identify and mitigate potential threats. This knowledge serves as a shield against online scams, ensuring that one does not fall prey to phishing attempts, identity theft, or financial fraud.

Additionally, cybersecurity education brings about a broader awareness of the psychological manipulation techniques used by malicious actors. By understanding these tactics, individuals can recognize and resist attempts to exploit their vulnerabilities, protecting themselves against scams and mind control techniques. This knowledge serves as a powerful tool in safeguarding personal and financial information.

Furthermore, the subchapter addresses the critical role of cybersecurity education in espionage and intelligence agencies. In an interconnected world, nations are engaged in a constant battle to protect their sensitive information. By advocating for cybersecurity education, this subchapter highlights the importance of training individuals in cybersecurity techniques, enhancing national security and averting potential cyber threats.

Overall, the advocacy for cybersecurity education and awareness is a call to action for the adult audience interested in the niches of A Web of Deceit, Cybersecurity and online scams, psychological manipulation and mind control, and Espionage and intelligence agencies. It emphasizes the need to equip individuals with the necessary knowledge to navigate the digital landscape safely. By promoting cybersecurity education, individuals can protect themselves from cyber threats, contributing to a safer and more secure online environment for all.

Legal frameworks and international cooperation against cybercrime

In today's interconnected world, where the internet plays a vital role in our daily lives, the threat of cybercrime looms large. Criminals and malicious actors have found new avenues to exploit unsuspecting individuals, governments, and organizations. As a result, legal frameworks and international cooperation have become crucial in the fight against cybercrime.

The emergence of the dark web, a hidden part of the internet accessible only through specialized software, has exacerbated the problem. Criminals on the dark web engage in various illicit activities, including selling personal information, hacking tools, drugs, and even engaging in human trafficking. To combat this growing menace, legal frameworks have been established to provide a solid foundation for law enforcement agencies to tackle cybercrime effectively.

Countries around the world have recognized the need for robust legislation to address cyber threats. These laws encompass a wide range of offenses, including hacking, identity theft, online fraud, and the dissemination of malicious software. By criminalizing these activities, governments aim to deter potential offenders and provide a means to prosecute those responsible.

However, cybercrime doesn't respect national borders. Criminals can operate from one country while targeting victims in another, making international cooperation paramount. Through mutual legal assistance treaties and international organizations such as Interpol and Europol, countries work together to exchange information, share best practices, and coordinate efforts to combat cybercrime.

Effective international cooperation against cybercrime involves the sharing of intelligence and evidence, joint investigation teams, and extradition agreements. This collaboration allows law enforcement agencies to track down and apprehend cybercriminals, dismantling their networks and disrupting their illicit activities.

In addition to legal frameworks and international cooperation, public awareness and education are vital in the fight against cybercrime. Individuals must be educated about the risks and vulnerabilities associated with online activities, enabling them to protect themselves and their personal information. Governments and organizations must also invest in cybersecurity measures to safeguard their systems and data from malicious attacks.

With cybercrime posing a significant threat to individuals, governments, and organizations alike, legal frameworks and international cooperation are indispensable tools in the ongoing battle against the dark side of the web. By strengthening legislation, fostering collaboration, and promoting awareness, we can create a safer digital environment for all. Together, we can combat cybercrime and protect our online world from deceit and manipulation.

The responsibility of individuals, organizations, and governments in securing the web

In this digital age, the web has become an integral part of our lives, connecting us to a world of information and opportunities. However, with the increasing reliance on the internet, there is also a rising threat of cybercrime, online scams, psychological manipulation, and espionage. It is crucial for individuals, organizations, and governments to take responsibility for securing the web and protecting themselves from the dangers lurking in the shadows.

Individuals play a vital role in securing the web. It is essential to maintain good cyber hygiene by using strong, unique passwords for every online account, enabling two-factor authentication, and regularly updating software and applications. By being vigilant and cautious while browsing the internet, individuals can avoid falling victim to online scams and phishing attempts. Additionally, individuals should educate themselves about the risks associated with sharing personal information online and exercise caution when interacting with unknown entities.

Organizations, especially those dealing with sensitive customer data, have a significant responsibility in securing the web. Implementing robust cybersecurity measures, such as firewalls, encryption, and intrusion detection systems, is crucial in safeguarding against cyber threats. Regular security audits and employee awareness training programs can further enhance an organization's ability to detect and prevent cyber-attacks. By prioritizing cybersecurity and investing in cutting-edge technology, organizations can create a safer online environment for their customers and employees.

Governments also bear the responsibility of securing the web. They must enact and enforce legislation that punishes cybercriminals and provides a legal framework for combating cyber threats. Governments should collaborate with international counterparts to share intelligence and develop strategies to counter cyber espionage and online scams. Additionally, allocating resources to support cybersecurity research and development can help in staying one step ahead of cybercriminals.

Web References

https://larsbirkeland.com/cyber-espionage/#:~:text=Cyber espionage can also pose a direct
threat,can cause widespread blackouts and disrupt daily life.

https://www.linkedin.com/pulse/unmasking-vishing-how-cybercriminals-exploiting-human

https://en.wikipedia.org/wiki/Dark_Web

https://www.linkedin.com/posts/wajid-nazir-05568a202_title-unraveling-the-web-of-deceit-adeep-activity-7090062763804254209-Rouo

https://blog.asecurity.in/navigating-the-dark-web-insights-into-the-underbelly-of-the-internet/

https://gogle.services/2023/07/26/the-evolving-landscape-of-cybersecurity-challenges-andsolutions/

https://blog.darkscan.app/an-introduction-to-the-dark-web-understanding-the-hiddeninternet

https://drjasonjones.com/dark_psychology/

https://211check.org/blog-the-psychology-behind-why-people-create-online-scams-and-fraud/

https://www.linkedin.com/pulse/ethics-online-anonymity-balancing-privacy-security-hagen

Reference

https://www.academia.edu/45629653/Dark_Web_A_Breeding_Gro
und_for_ID_Thefts_and_Fi
nancial_Crimes#:~:text=The explosion of the internet has given
rise,and the number of
unsuspecting victims is growing.

https://www.linkedin.com/pulse/cybersecurity-dark-web-
understanding-threat-landscapemohit-singh

https://www.linkedin.com/pulse/cyber-espionage-geopolitics-how-
virtual-spies-shape-worlderic-ford

http://www.indiandefencereview.com/spotlights/role-of-
intelligence-agencies-in-modernwarfare/

https://www.idenfy.com/blog/ways-fraudsters-commit-identity-
theft/

https://www.linkedin.com/pulse/exploring-dark-recesses-web-bev-
robb

https://www.linkedin.com/pulse/navigating-evolving-landscape-
cybersecurity-guide-stayingahmad

https://academic.oup.com/isq/article/65/1/146/6103943

https://www.forbes.com/sites/forbestechcouncil/2021/02/16/demy
stifying-the-dark-web/

https://link.springer.com/article/10.1007/s11896-019-09334-5

https://www.unodc.org/southasia/frontpage/2012/May/india_-
addressing-the-rise-ofcybercrime-amongst-children.html

https://www.hrw.org/report/2016/05/25/stifling-
dissent/criminalization-peaceful-expressionindia

https://www.linkedin.com/pulse/dark-web-stories-how-30-enables-
new-generationanonymity-unhale

https://www.linkedin.com/pulse/navigating-digital-tightrope-
balancing-national-securitycummins

Reference

https://www.weforum.org/reports/global-risks-report-2022/in-full/chapter-3-digitaldependencies-and-cyber-vulnerabilities

https://arxiv.org/abs/2006.08342

https://www.freecodecamp.org/news/how-to-use-artificial-intelligence-in-cybersecurity/

https://aware.eccouncil.org/11-best-ways-to-stop-scammers-with-security-awareness.html

https://www.frontiersin.org/articles/10.3389/fcomp.2021.563060/full

https://www.weforum.org/agenda/2021/09/to-fight-cybercrime-we-need-to-understand-itseconomics/

https://www.isaca.org/resources/isaca-journal/issues/2021/volume-2/the-dark-web-and-therole-of-secure-human-behaviors

https://www.cmu.edu/iso/aware/dont-take-the-bait/social-engineering.html

https://cisomag.com/tech-tip-how-to-avoid-online-scams/

https://wesecureapp.com/blog/ai-generated-phishing-emails/

https://www.linkedin.com/pulse/social-engineering-attacks-recognizing-defending-againstmanipulative

https://www.linkedin.com/pulse/online-scams-protecting-yourself-digital-wild

https://study.com/learn/lesson/power-suggestion-psychology-examples.html

https://www.vadesecure.com/en/blog/pretexting-5-examples-of-social-engineering-tactics

Reference

https://www.chegg.com/homework-help/questions-and-answers/1-problem-delvemysterious-world-hessians-developed-ludwig-otto-hesse-incidentally-student-q57454905

https://thehackpost.com/pros-and-cons-of-online-anonymity.html

https://www.keepersecurity.com/blog/2023/06/21/how-cybercriminals-are-using-ai-forcyberattacks/#:~:text=Instead   of writing their own phishing emails or,and style. This makes the scam more believable.

https://link.springer.com/chapter/10.1057/978-1-137-56894-6_8/cover

https://www.dqindia.com/dark-web-underbelly-internet-subset-deep-web/

https://www.pewresearch.org/global/2022/12/06/views-of-social-media-and-its-impacts-onsociety-in-advanced-economies-2022/

https://c9lab.com/blog/understanding-the-psychology-behind-phishing-scams/

https://www.businesstechweekly.com/operational-efficiency/business-continuity/cyberresilience-vs-cyber-security/

https://www.linkedin.com/pulse/psychology-phishing-attacks-cognitive-biases-emotionalebrahim-ranama#:~:text=Phishing attacks use emotional manipulation to elicit specific,tactic
called "amygdala hijacking" to manipulate their victims.

https://nsarchive.gwu.edu/briefing-book/intelligence/2019-03-04/understanding-cia-howcovert-overt-operations-proposed-approved-during-cold-war

https://phoenixnap.com/blog/strong-great-password-ideas#:~:text=Has a combination of
upper and lowercase letters,example, look at these two passwords:
89&^598
ILoveMyCatLordStewart

Reference

https://www.researchgate.net/publication/363415520_How_the_Pr
esence_of_Cognitive_Bias
es_in_Phishing_Emails_Affects_Human_Decision-making

https://iasbaba.com/2016/02/1-intelligence-agencies-play-a-vital-
role-in-securing-theterritory-of-india-from-terrorism-drug-
trafficking-and-illegal-arms-trade-however-recentattack-in-
pathankot-has-exposed-the-weakness-of-i/

https://www.sciencedirect.com/science/article/pii/S0022000014000
178

https://www.researchgate.net/publication/329367473_DarkWeb_C
yber_Threat_Intelligence_From_Data_to_Intelligence_to_Prediction

https://www.chathamhouse.org/2022/02/what-cyber-attack

https://ludwig.guru/s/aims to shed light on

https://www.scirp.org/journal/paperinformation.aspx?paperid=111
804